200
6x

A THOUSAND YEARS
OF LONDON BRIDGE

Dedicated to
HAROLD K. KING,
C.B.E., C.Eng., F.I.C.E., F.I. Mun.E.,
City Engineer, Corporation of London,
to whom we owe the new London Bridge

A THOUSAND YEARS OF LONDON BRIDGE

C. W. SHEPHERD

JOHN BAKER LONDON

HASTINGS HOUSE NEW YORK

© 1971 *C. W. Shepherd*

Published in 1971 by
John Baker (Publishers) Ltd
5 Royal Opera Arcade
Pall Mall, London SW1

ISBN 0 212 98395 4

First American edition
published in 1971 by
Hastings House, Publishers, Inc.
New York, N.Y. 10016

ISBN 8038 5368 8

Library of Congress Catalog Card Number
74 163183

Printed in Great Britain by
*Staples Printers Limited at their
Rochester, Kent, establishment*

CONTENTS

ILLUSTRATIONS

PLATES

FIGURES IN THE TEXT

FOREWORD

This book is not put forward as a complete account of the succession of bridges which have culminated in our latest London Bridge. The reader may rightly ask why is not *this* or *that* included? The answer is that a subject so outstretched over time, so woven with detail, yet so barely documented cannot be compressed into a book of this length without its becoming categorical and shorn of much romance. It has been my aim to highlight the colourful side of our old friend through the changing scenes of its existence, during which it has played an important part in the history of London City. *Knight's London* could not have put it better than it did in 1851:

"In the annals of the metropolis, at least, if not the whole kingdom, London Bridge has been one of the most famous of our public monuments for not far short of a thousand years."

This quotation from the past is not the only one which will be encountered in the following pages. Historians depend upon books. Even the giants of that learned breed have culled their facts from previous writers, and it is obvious that Gibbon did not live in Rome when he wrote of the decline and fall of that empire, any more than did Macaulay witness the stirring sight of Horatius Cocles holding the Tiber bridge against Lars Porsena. The best example of an on-the-spot historian is surely old John Stow, who wrote more of what he saw than what he read, and as part of my indebtedness to him I have paid a small tribute in my last chapter, which I have called "A London Bridge Miscellany".

Of the Miscellany I would say this: where some compelling subject or occasion does not fit precisely into any chapter I have reserved it for the Miscellany, there to treat it separately on its merits. Thus the Scotland *versus* England joust-of-honour on London Bridge might just have found a place in our chapter on pageantry, though slightly incongruously, so its story appears in its own right in the London Bridge Miscellany. Therefore the Miscellany is not a collection of after-thoughts.

The same convenient chapter gives space to details of the famous Thames-driven water-works which supplied water to the City and Southwark almost with the efficiency of a modern Water Board!

It may be thought that I have made too much of Southwark, that somewhat dreary borough on the south side of the bridge. Yet Southwark, to which I have given a full chapter, has played a great part in the history of both bridge and City – some of it far from salubrious, and far from dreary. The dreariness, if such it be, came at a period nearer our time. As for the in-salubrity of old, the reader may form his own conclusions when he reads in Chapter 8 of the Borough being a safe retreat for the City's rogues, being then outside the latter's jurisdiction. Then there was its concentration of "stews" (otherwise brothels) loaned by the lord mayor of London to a set of Dutch harpies.

That is one aspect of the picture of old Southwark. Another presents the twelfth-century cathedral, regarded by some as the finest medieval religious building in London after Westminster Abbey. Standing a hundred paces from the south end of London Bridge, it is familiar to the thousands of commuters who daily use the railway station of that name. Southwark Cathedral is of intense interest to Americans because of its association with the Southwark-born John Harvard who left this country from Southwark in 1637 for America, there to found what ultimately came to be called Harvard University. He is commemorated in the Harvard Chapel of the cathedral, rebuilt and so named by the university itself (plate 6).

Add to this that John Harvard's father, Robert, was a friend of Shakespeare (who lived in Southwark) and met John's mother-to-be in Stratford on Avon in the company of the Bard himself, and there seems ample reason for our dwelling on Southwark as we have done. No wonder American visitors to this country flock to Southwark to pick up the trail of John Harvard – and Shakespeare.

I have tried to follow the history of our London Bridge from the first timber structures to the present erection in Arizona, and it has been a history of great consequence, embracing much that is dear to the citizens of a great city.

Perhaps our historical climax was the revolutionary removal of the houses on Old London Bridge, the bridge of Peter de Colechurch, which spanned the Thames for some 650 years before it was entirely replaced by the Rennies' structure, much of which now stands at Lake Havasu City in far-off Arizona. Some details of this startling transference will be found in Chapter 11 which also deals briefly with the ultimate bridge of all.

The widely-held belief in the existence of a Roman London Bridge has inevitably cropped up and, I hope, been reasonably treated. Old Thames has seen various London Bridges in its day, but it is our belief that a Roman-built bridge was not one of them.

However, since Father Thames has been the sole reason for all London Bridges, old and new, it seems fitting that we should devote our first chapter to him, and him only.

I

———◦◉◦———

LONDON'S RIVER

Who shall say what ages have passed since a little spring in the Cotswolds began its trickle towards where London was yet to be? We know that the sparkling brooklet pursued its way, joined here and there by other streams, widening itself with the pastoral miles, through wood and through meadow, until men called it not a brook but a river. On and on it flowed through the early Oxford where folk gave it the name of Thamesis, soon to be cut to Thames, leaving the latter part to be turned into Isis which is one name for the Thames at Oxford to this day.

The actual source of the Thames presents as complex a problem as is set by any map. Even the local folk around the reputed sources still argue about it. Some say this; some say that. It is held by many that Seven Springs out Cheltenham way is the source, and that the little river Churn there is really the beginning of the Thames itself, though this presents yet another problem – which of the "Seven Springs" is the true beginning of the river Churn.

Another theory is that the Thames begins at Thames Head in a meadow at Coates, near the village of Kemble, a few miles from Gloucester. That the controversy is not new is shown by the poet and novelist Thomas Love Peacock, who took a hand in it. Peacock, whose writings graced the first half of the nineteenth century, made a special study of the Thames. Here is his verdict on the location of its source: "The infant river in Kemble Meadow is never totally dry [i.e. as Thames Head is sometimes dry] and to the source by which the stream is *constantly* supplied can alone belong the honour of giving birth to the Thames."

By the time we reach Cricklade all doubts have ceased. The river is emphatically the Thames and, except that it is called the Isis at Oxford, remains the Thames until its muddied waters

have passed under London Bridge on its way to the North
Sea, the salt water of which has met it at tidal intervals as far
up its course as Teddington.

After flowing through the little town of Lechlade, the ever-
widening Thames goes majestically on his way, fed first by this
stream and then that until the better known tributaries appear
in the names of Kennet, Evenlode, Windrush, Mole and others,
including, at Oxford, the Cherwell with its nostalgic pull on
"Oxford men" the world over.

> *At Reading once arrived, clear Kennet overtakes*
> *Her lord, the stately Thames – which that great flood again*
> *With many signs of joy doth entertain,*
> *Then Lodden next comes in, contributing her store,*
> *As still we see, the much runs ever to the more.*

The poet was Michael Drayton, a friend of Shakespeare and
well known in the Southwark area around London Bridge.

Which brings us to Reading, more famous today for its
biscuits than its history – of which it has a rich store. Here is a
gem from the latter, from Fuller's *Church History* (1655):

"As King Henry VIII was hunting in Windsor Forest, he
was either casually lost, or more probably losing himself, struck
down, about dinner-time, to the Abbey of Reading, where,
disguising himself . . . he was invited to the abbot's table, and
passed for one of the king's guard. . . . A sirloin of beef was
set before him (so knighted, saith tradition, by this Henry):
on which the king laid lustily. . . . 'Well fare thy heart,' quoth
the abbot, 'and here in a cup of sack I remember the health of
his grace your master. I would give an hundred pounds on the
condition I could feed so lustily on beef as you. Alas! my weak
and squeezie stomach will hardly digest the wing of a small
chicken.' The king pledged him . . . and departed as undis-
covered as he came hither.

"Some weeks later the abbot was sent for by a pursuivant,
brought to London by river under London Bridge, clapt in the
Tower and fed for a short time on bread and water.

"The abbot was sore puzzled as to how he had incurred the
king's displeasure, but:

"At last a sirloin of beef was set before him, of which the

abbot fed as the farmer of his grange, and verified the proverb
that 'two hungry meals makes the third a glutton'.

" 'My Lord,' quoth the King (who had watched him
secretly), 'presently deposit your hundred pounds in gold, or
else no going hence all the daies of your life. . . . I have been
your physician to cure you of your squeezie stomach, and here,
as I deserve, I demand my fee for the same.' The abbot, glad
that he had escaped so, returned by river to Reading, as somewhat lighter in purse, so much more merry in heart, than when
he came thence."

To disbelievers of this story I offer a hint of caution. The
ruins of a Benedictine abbey, founded by Henry I, are still to
be seen in Reading.

Soon we must begin to view the Thames with special respect
for, on reaching Windsor, it becomes a royal river, and begins
to show itself as a definite part of English history, with Windsor
Castle towering above it. It was here that King John stayed
while the Barons were preparing for him to sign the Magna
Carta at Runnymeade on the historic meadow a few miles
below on the left bank of the Thames.

At Windsor even the swans belong to the Crown, and have
done since the time of Edward III, whose ancestor, Richard I,
introduced *cygnus* to this country from Cyprus. You will see
swans all down the river, even at London Bridge where they
waddle and wallow about the muddy shore at low tide, and
sail majestically when the river is high (plate 25). But the
London Bridge swans (and some farther up the river) are not
royal swans; they belong to the Dyers' and Vintners' companies
of the City of London. The last annual count of the Vintners'
swans as I write (1969) was 209.

The royalty of the river greets us again at Hampton Court,
that imposing and ancient pile so closely connected with
Cardinal Wolsey. He it was who bought the already centuries
old Hampton manor, and on the site built his luxurious palace.
He it was who later "surprised the Thames" by the unparal-
leled panoply of his retinue when he passed over old London
Bridge to make a somewhat meddlesome visit to France.*

Wolsey lived in regal state at Hampton Court until jealousy

* This remarkable scene is described in Chapter 5

in high places prompted him to present it to his royal master, Henry VIII, who made it his residence, as did other monarchs after him. It is tempting to dwell on this great palace which has earned its place in modern history as a tourist attraction. Were we to dwell upon it we should find ourselves discovering that King Edward VI (son of Henry VIII) was born there and that his mother, Jane Seymour, died there a few days after his birth, and that Catherine Howard, Henry's fifth wife, was disgraced there, and that there shortly afterwards he married Catherine Parr. At this palace Charles I and the very young Henrietta Maria spent their honeymoon after their lively progress under London Bridge, described elsewhere in this book. There too James I conducted the Prayer Book Conference and the Authorised Version of the Bible was started on its way.

In due course the Thames takes London town upon itself, and it is worth taking a look at its colourful history during the earlier centuries of its association with the capital.

Gone today are the river sports regularly watched by crowds on both banks and particularly from London Bridge which must

Fig. 1. A Thames boat-joust in action: after a manuscript drawing.

have been made of sturdy stuff to stand the swaying pressure, particularly in the case of the first timber bridge. Among these sports were jousting with lances between the occupants of rival rowing wherries, and the water quintain which meant tilting at a target capable of swinging a sand-bag round and knocking the contestant into the river, which it did more often than not, to the delight of the spectators.

There was plenty of activity to be seen on the Thames in

those early days, even from the old timber bridge. Stow tells us that in his day and before there were no fewer than 2,000 wherries darting about the river on their lawful occasions and that they gave employment to a corresponding number of watermen. All this, it seems, was related to the Thames between London Bridge and Westminster, the latter then being a separate city. The road between Westminster and the City, or such road as there was, was unmade and followed a winding way through the village of Charing.

Along the Strand (which *was* a strand in those days) stood many great houses of the nobility. Now they are gone or rebuilt and put to other purposes, though their names still cling to them and recall those agreeable days, as witness Somerset House built by the Lord Protector Somerset, acting during the regency of the young Edward VI. (Somerset filched much of the stone for his purpose by pulling down Pardon Haugh Church, a burial place adjacent to St Paul's, so it may not come amiss to know that he ended his days on the block at Tower Hill.)

All these great houses had their "water-gates" at the ends of their gardens, from which the owners stepped into their private barges or hired Thames wherries to make visits up and down the river, particularly to the City and the Tower, which was at times a royal residence.

But there were those, during three centuries, to whom the beauties of the silent highway could have offered no pleasure. The Thames was the road by which the victim of despotism came from the Tower to Westminster Hall, in most cases to return to his barge "with the edge of the axe turned against his face". They had passed below London Bridge for the last time. Thus there were the two dukes of Buckingham, father and son, who were executed at the Tower. The second duke had been rowed up the Thames from Traitors' Gate, open to the river from the fortress, to stand his trial at Westminster Hall where he was sentenced to death. When he stepped into his barge after the trial he saw the boatmen and others arranging silken cushions which had accommodated him on the way upstream.

"No, no," he protested. "When I came hither I was the Duke of Buckingham, but see, the axe-blade is pointed towards me. I am no longer he. Indeed I am less than you, for I go back to die."

The significance of the axe-blade's direction did not die out with the axe, for, in certain modern courts martial, the accused on returning to the chamber, knows the verdict by the position of his sword on the table. If it is pointing towards him the verdict is adverse; if the hilt is towards him, the reverse applies, and no doubt the officer picks it up with alacrity!

We would have to search for many forgotten records to describe the London Thames as a royal highway, for such was the stretch between the Tower and Westminster, partly for the reason that royal progressions were so frequent as to go unrecorded. We do know, however, that on all occasions London Bridge, as well as the shores, was well crowded, which makes us wonder how news of a progression got around when there were no newspapers or other methods of instant communication. Clearly word-of-mouth had its own wings.

One of the "best attended" processions was on the occasion when Henrietta Maria of France came from France to be met downriver by our Charles I, having been married to him by proxy the previous year. Here is one account of the progress as culled from an observer's notes at the time:

"The king and queen in the royal barge, with many other barges of honour and thousands of boats, passed through London Bridge to Whitehall; Infinite numbers, besides these, in wherries, standing in houses, ships, lighters, western barges, and on each side of the shore. . . ."

Of course, the popular importance of all this was the high romance which surrounded it. Henrietta Maria was the daughter of Henry IV of France and was only fifteen when she was married to Charles by proxy in 1624, Charles still being the heir-apparent at the age of twenty-four. In 1625 he ascended the throne. Little wonder that the citizens of London crowded to see their new king as he came downriver to meet and return with his young queen.

As one might imagine, the watermen of whom Stow wrote were not without their "characters"; indeed the same applies today, except that there are not so many of them. Yet you may look into more than one riverside inn near London Bridge today and discover men who might well have stepped out of W. W. Jacobs' stories. In those early days of the London Thames there was one who surpassed all others as a notability. John Taylor became known as the Water-poet, though only a wherry-man, and you may find his name, after three centuries, in modern reference books. He worked on the Thames, operating from Southwark near London Bridge, and it has been suggested that on many occasions he had the fortune to ferry Shakespeare whose Globe Theatre was near by.

As a waterman he was grateful to the Thames for his living and, as a poet, he put that gratitude into words:

> *But noble Thames, whilst I can hold a pen,*
> *I will disclose thy glory unto men;*
> *Thou in the morning when my coin is scant*
> *Before the evening doth supply my want.*

As a youth he was apprenticed to a Thames waterman, after which the navy claimed him and he saw service at the siege of Cadiz. Eventually he returned to his beloved Thames and took up his old occupation as a wherry-man and a writer of rugged, racy verse. An account of him appears in Southey's "Observations on Uneducated Poets". Further, the Spenser Society reprinted a number of his verses as recently as 1870.

His last years as a waterman were clouded by unforeseen circumstances, for this old river trade became threatened by the private coaches which sprang into being almost without warning, a happening not unlike the ousting of the stage coaches by the railways some centuries later. "This infernal swarm of coaches have overrun the land that we can get no living on the water," Taylor wrote bitterly. "They have undone my poor trade. I do affirm that, especially if the Court be at Whitehall, they do rob us of our livings, and carry some five hundred and sixty fares from us daily." The Thames was ceasing to be the "silent highway" and for a time John Taylor championed the cause of the watermen, but he fought a hopeless battle; eventually he gave up the river and took over a tavern and died a popular inn-keeper.

Lest he be thought of as a purveyor of doggerel (like the later McGonnagle, the Scottish "poet" of renown) here is a little gem which has been remembered for three centuries:

Thou sayest that Poetry descended is
From Poverty; thou tak'st thy mark amiss.
In spite of weal or woe, or want of pelf,
It is a kingdom of content itself.

Of course there remained much work for the watermen a few hundred yards downriver from London Bridge, at Bermondsey, where stood an abbey of Cluniac monks, founded in the eleventh century. Reminders of this religious institution may still be met with in such names as Paradise Street, St Saviour's Wharf, Cherry Garden Pier, Salutation Wharf, Angel Inn and others. A few watermen live there to this day, earning their undefinable living. One of them has a cottage in Paradise Street, the wash-house of which is overrun by a rambling grape-vine, whose father vine, I suspect, was of monastic origin. At least I liked to think so when this waterman recently gave me an enormous basket of little grapes from which I made six bottles of a presentable Sauternes-like white wine.

2

THE FIRST BRIDGE

There is nothing enviable in casting doubt on an accepted legend. Nor is there about accepting a legend for its own sake, which one would have to do in giving the Romans credit for building the first bridge across the Thames from London City. Therefore one approaches this subject with caution, for it seems impossible to find firm evidence of any such bridge; and, surely, had there been one, there would have been many references to it by early writers. But even John Stow, that old boon and blessing to London historians, makes no mention of a Roman bridge across the Thames at London. Nor yet does one find such in that estimable old work the *Chronicles of London Bridge*.

Yet there is much in old books about the timber bridge which spanned the river, built in or about A.D. 944 by the good priests of Southwark, including Peter de Colechurch, whose church of the same name stood in Poultry on the north side of the river. This was but five hundred years after the Romans departed, leaving their bridge – if any. In retrospect this is not a long period, as witness the longevity of the first stone London Bridge (begun but not finished by the same Peter de Colechurch) which lasted for six and a half centuries – until, indeed, the building of our granite London Bridge in the enlightened years of the early nineteenth century. Surely any Roman bridge, standing at the time of their departure, could not have disappeared without trace, yet trace was never found though the Romans built well in stone as the remains of Hadrian's Wall still testify.

In 1214 there came a great drought to the south of England which particularly affected the Thames, to the extent that "men walked dryshod" across most of its width by London

Bridge, the foundations of which were easily examined; but there were no traces of a Roman bridge.

Opinions are conflicting and have been made more so by the discovery, as recently as 1969, of the finest stretch of Roman road in London. The find was made between Southwark Cathedral and the river. This has been regarded in many quarters to have been the approach to the Roman bridge, if such there were, a little upstream of our own familiar bridge and its predecessors. Hitherto the possible site of the Roman bridge was thought to be downstream, owing to Roman coins and other objects being found strewn about the river-bed; but more recent excavations have divulged rubbish pits and a well where the approach road would have been. But the archaeologists, proud, as they might well be, of their new find of an approach road, have nothing to say about an actual Roman bridge.

Could it have been that this approach road led to a landing point for Roman boats carrying troops and others to and fro across the river? Or could there have been a succession of pontoon bridges of an impermanent nature?

The first regular communication between London City and Southwark was by ferry, and, for a period, by one ferry only, a ferry of some renown for, because of it, the first timber bridge across the Thames was built, and Stow quotes as his authority one Bartholomew Linstead, or Fowle, the last prior of St Mary Overie church in Southwark. The ferry was worked by a John Audery (or Overs) who, it seems, had several boats on the site, all of them perpetually busy, whereby he amassed a great fortune; but more of that anon.

The most authentic account of John Audery is contained in a pamphlet or tract (call it what you will) actually printed on London Bridge. It bears the imprint: "Printed for T. Harris at the Looking Glass, on London Bridge, and sold by C. Corbet at Addison's Head in Fleet Street, 1744. Price 6d." (The addresses of the printer and bookseller are significant of the old practice of giving shop-signs a visual appeal by means of a symbol. Illiteracy was common in those days and one can imagine an employer sending a messenger to deliver a letter or parcel to so-and-so at the Looking Glass or the Addison's Head, an address on which the messenger could scarcely go wrong. Others were the Dog and Pot, the Judge's Head, the Wheel, the Black Boy, the Three Bibles, the Golden Globe, the Bird in Cage, and so on.)

The preamble to the tract above mentioned is interesting. "The True History [it runs] of the Life and sudden Death of old John Overs, the rich Ferryman of London, shewing how he lost his life by his own covetousness. And of his Daughter Mary, who caused the Church of St Mary Overs in Southwark to be built; and of the building of London Bridge." After some lengthy, moralistic outpourings the pamphlet settles down to its story:

"Before there was any Bridge at all built over the Thames there was only a Ferry, to which divers boats belonged, to transport all passengers betwixt Southwark and Churchyard Alley, that being the high-road way between Middlesex and Sussex, and London. This Ferry was rented of the City, by one John Overs, which he enjoyed for many years together, to his great profit; for it is to be imagined that no small benefit could arise from the ferrying over footmen, horsemen, all manner of cattle, all market folks that came with provisions to the City, strangers and others."

Overs, however, though he kept several servants and apprentices, was of "so covetous a soul, that notwithstanding that he possessed an estate equal to that of the best Alderman in London, acquired by unceasing labour, and usury, yet his habit and dwelling were both strongly expressive of the most miserable poverty". He had an only daughter "of a most beautiful aspect and a pious disposition, whom he had cared to see well and liberally educated, though at the cheapest rate; and yet so, when she grew ripe and mature for marriage, he would suffer no man of what condition or quality soever, by his good will, to have sight of her, much less than access unto her."

A young gallant (so the story runs) who seems to have thought more of being the waterman's heir than his son-in-law, took the opportunity, whilst the father was engaged at the ferry, to be admitted to her company. The first interview, we are told, "pleased well; the second better; but the third concluded the match between them".

All this, of course, was unknown to the miserly John Overs,

who continued his ways as before. But Nemeses watching carefully saw that he got his deserts, which he did by a mean and stupid act of his own. Seeking to save the cost of a day's upkeep of his household he decided to feign himself dead for twenty-four hours, for it was customary at the time for no food to be taken while the master's body lay in the house. He acted the part well, even to the extent of whitening his face to a corpse-like tone. And so he lay there beneath a sheet with candles flickering about him. He had, of course, achieved his daughter's compliance.

But alas, the servants were in no mood for lamentation over so mean a master. On the contrary, they dragged out all the food from the cupboards and had a sing-song to mark the occasion. John Overs, of course, listened to all this with anything but corpse-like calm. At last he rose in his bed, only to be struck really dead by the hammer of a menial who thought the Devil was rising up in his master's body. But this was not the end of the story as it concerns John Overs, his ferry, his wealth, his daughter or the timber London Bridge so soon to be erected.

When the young gallant seeking Mary's heart and the old man's money heard of the ferryman's untimely end he lost no time in setting out for London by horse from his home in the country. But he was destined not to see Mary again, for his horse stumbled and threw him on to the rough highway so that he broke his neck. Thus Mary had a second bereavement, even before she had decided where her father's remains should be laid. Eventually she gained permission from the monks of Bermondsey Abbey to inter him in the abbey precincts. The prior of the abbey, who was absent at the time, and who disapproved thoroughly of John Overs, was curious about the new grave on his return. Hearing who was the occupant of it, he flew into a rage and ordered the body to be taken up forthwith. Overs, apart from his bad character as a usurer and extortionist, was also under excommunication. So says the tract published at the Looking Glass on London Bridge. The prior had the body tied to the back of his donkey, the animal being turned out of the monastery to do as he pleased with his melancholy load, though not before the prior had asked God to direct the animal to some place fitting for such a character.

The ass made his way to a plot of land where stood one of the many gibbets which were about London in those days. Here the ass shook off his load and walked back to the abbey. As for John Overs, he was duly buried at the spot where the donkey had left him, a fitting place as the prior no doubt observed. So much for the "Looking Glass" tract which, by the way, is available for inspection at the British Museum.

We must now return to Mary who, under the terms of her father's will, had become an exceedingly rich woman. The two tragedies in her early life, mentioned above, naturally affected her greatly, and in two ways: she wished to withdraw from the life around her, and to forget it if possible; and she wished to escape from the so-called suitors, otherwise fortune-hunters, who soon began to plague her existence. She was a religious girl, and to religion she turned for solace and protection. With the money at her disposal and the regular profits of the ferry she was able to found a house of sisters, where the east part of St Mary Overie church later stood, and where Southwark Cathedral (the cathedral church of St Saviour) now stands near the end of London Bridge – familiar to the many thousands of commuters who use London Bridge station daily, and to the regular ebb and flow of people between the City and Southwark. The convent was turned into a college for priests by Swithun, bishop of Winchester in the ninth century as we shall read in our chapter on Southwark.

It is said by some that the first timber bridge across the Thames was put up by Peter of Colechurch, a chaplain of the church St Mary Colechurch in Poultry, destroyed in the Great Fire of London. But it is more likely that the good priest Peter only had a hand in rebuilding the *last* timber bridge before the first stone one, which he initiated and began to build before he died, and that earlier timber bridges on the site (a little east of subsequent bridges) had been put up and destroyed. A glance at the history of this timber bridge gives us an idea of the impermanence of such bridges. It was swept away by flood in 1091 and quickly rebuilt, destroyed by fire, then again by floods, then by ice-packs and by fire again. (This is taking no note of the maulings it received from successive Danish marauders.)

Yet the very impermanence of a timber bridge had its

advantages. It could be repaired or even rebuilt in a short time, for the piles on which it was built were generally un-impaired, and on these the citizens, both of the City and Southwark, got promptly to work. The priests of Southwark were particularly helpful in securing money for the work and, often, lending their own labour to the job.

It must not be thought that the first London Bridge was a sketchy contrivance, for it was described in an account of the Thames invasion of the Danes, in particular that of King Sweyn of Denmark, as having turrets and roofed bulwarks and a generally impressive (for those days) appearance. This applies also to the reconstructed timber bridges that followed, including the last timber bridge built by Peter de Colechurch.

This Peter de Colechurch is a strange figure in the history of the first London Bridge, and he flits through the records like some phantom of architecture. Try as you may, you will not discover how a chaplain of a church in Poultry (St Mary Colechurch) gained such architectural skill as to put him in the front rank of those early builders of bridges over the wide and often turbulent Thames. As we learn that those bridges had their inception on the Southwark side of the river it seems clear that the good Peter must have frequently left his church in Poultry (continuous with Cheapside today) to work with, and perhaps inspire, the pious priests on the other side of the river, the priests of the college of canons which sprang in-directly from the bequests of Mary Audery.

Be that as it may, the pious Peter's name is linked in all records with, not only the timber bridge, but with the stone bridge which followed it – the bridge on which were built houses, a chapel and many other things besides, as we shall see later.

The first timber bridge, before Peter de Colechurch came upon the scene, met with disasters which were not due to be discontinued. For:

"On the sixteenth of November, the feast of St Edmund the Archbishop, in the year 1091, at the hour of six, a dreadful whirlwind from the South-East, coming from Africa, blew upon the City, and overthrew upwards of six hundred houses, several churches, greatly damaged the Tower, and tore away the roof and part of the wall of the Church of St Mary le Bow, in Cheapside."

Some historians say that it was Peter de Colechurch's bridge which was demolished, but the more reliable accounts have it otherwise. In any case there was plenty coming to Peter's bridge. I have mentioned fires, storms and floods, and shall mention them again; they were, one supposes, "acts of God" and men applied a certain amount of philosophy to them and implacably restored or rebuilt their London Bridge. But one could not apply much philosophy to the Danes, who, over varying periods, continually attacked London, usually from the Thames. Ethelred the Unready endeavoured to buy off the Danes with the proceeds of a tax called the Danegeld which, in other words, was a levy on land per hide. There are several romantic explanations of the word "hide", a unit of land for the computation of tax. One of them is that it was as much land as its owner could encompass with strips of one cow's hide. Romantic as this may seem, it is rubbish. A hide was the name applied to a certain number of acres. It varied somewhat with locality and period. Thus, it varied from about two shillings in Anglo-Saxon times (when it originated) to six shillings in the time of the Conqueror, who revived it after a long lapse, though, of course, he had no cause to worry about the Danes whose attacks on England had long since ceased. We may note that an acre of today is 4,840 square yards but it varied considerably in olden times. Also we may note the value of money in Ethelred's day. A labourer received something like sixpence a week, so the Danegeld was no fleabite to those who had to pay it.

The Romans had left Britain in approximately A.D. 418 and their going was to prove an opportunity for many who had so far not dared to try to raid our land. Britain was soon subjected to attacks from the Picts in the north, the Scots from the north-west and the Saxons from the east. Then came the Danes, the sea-warriors known as the Vikings, remorseless fighters and pillagers by nature. We need apply ourselves here only to their activities concerning London and its timber bridge.

Here, then, is a note of our old friend Stow, in the first few words of which we cannot fail to detect a diffidence not normally associated with this doyen of London historians. "But first of the timber bridge," he writes in his Survey, "*the antiquity thereof being great, but uncertain;* [my italics] I remember to have read that in the year of Christ 994, Sweyn, king of Denmark, besieging the city of London, both by water and by land, the citizens defended themselves and their king Ethelred, so as part of their enemies were slain in battle, and part of them were drowned in the river Thames, because in their hasty rage they took no heed of the bridge."

This, of course, refers to the bridge we have already mentioned, but there is an amusing footnote to an annotated version of the Survey which indicates a much earlier bridge. It refers to a passage in Mr. Kemble's introduction to the first volume of his *Codex Diplomaticus aevi Saxonici*, in which he speaks of a woman, who being condemned to death for aiming at the life of a nobleman by means of witchcraft, and the sticking of pins into a waxen image, was executed by drowning at London Bridge. This, the writer of the footnote rightly concludes, shows that there was a timber bridge in the century before the bridge mentioned by Stow.

There is also an account of how, long prior to this, King Olave, or Anlaf, of Norway sailed up the river with a large fleet and reached Staines, which he sacked. In this account there is no mention of his encountering any bridge across the river, which indicates one of two things – that there was no bridge there or that Olave chose a time when an existing bridge was out of use owing to enemy action or an act of God, both of which seemed always to be round the corner.

Soon the Danish hordes were in possession of most of England including London and Sudrvirki, otherwise Southwark. King Ethelred fled to France, having failed in an attempt to carry London Bridge, now in possession of the Danes. Meanwhile, Olave and his fleet were lurking farther down the river. Later Ethelred returned to England to muster an army and try once more to oust the Danes.

A surprise awaited Ethelred in finding that his old enemy Olave had been converted to Christianity and was eager to side with him against the Danes. In due course Olave was canonised and took his place in the Calendar of saints, which accounts for the church of St Olave near London Bridge, and others of the same name which have now disappeared.

Failing in his new attempt to expel the Danes, Ethelred called a council of chiefs, and it was here that Olave offered to attack London Bridge with his fleet, provided Ethelred would join in his activities on land.

This was agreed to, and Olave set about planning his attack which shows us what a little ingenuity could do in those days. Here is one account of the matter:

"The proposition having been adopted, the necessary pre-parations were set about on all hands; and the first thing King Olave did was to direct some old houses to be pulled down, and with the wooden poles and twigs of osier thence obtained, to raise upon each of his ships a huge scaffolding, extending over the sides of the vessel, so as to enable the men to reach the enemy with their swords without coming from under cover; and at the same time, as he imagined, of such strength as to resist any stones that might be thrown down upon them from the upper works of the bridge. When everything was in readi-ness, both on the river and on shore, the ships rowed towards the bridge against the tide; but, as soon as they got near to it, they were assailed with so furious a shower of missiles and great stones, that, notwithstanding Olave's ingenious basket-work, not only helmets and shields gave way, but even some of the ships were sorely shattered, so that a considerable number of the men made off with themselves altogether. On this, driven to their last shifts, Olave and his brave Norsemen, rowing close up to the bridge, bound their barks with ropes and cables to the piles on which it was supported, and then, tugging their oars with all their might, and being assisted by the tide (we now see why they chose to make their attack while it was ebbing), they soon felt the fabric yielding to their efforts, and in no long time had the satisfaction of bringing down piers and bridge with one great crash into the water – the loads of stones that had been collected upon it, with the crowd of its armed defenders, only helping to make the ruin more complete. Great numbers of the Danes were drowned; those who could, fled, some to London, some to Southwark."

The bridge which was so ingeniously dealt with by Olave

was, of course, of timber, which meant that it was not long before Londoners and the men of Southwark had it up again. These London bridges, it should be said, were wide enough "to let two carriages pass one another". The building or re-building of such bridges, though lightly referred to in history (and in this book), must have cost a good deal of someone's money, but it is difficult to discover exactly whose. The best pointer seems to come from Stow,* who, in his *Survey of London*, says on one occasion: "Thus much for the old timber bridge, maintained partly by the proper lands, thereof, partly by the liberality of divers persons, and partly by taxation in divers shires, have I proved for the space of 215 years before the bridge of stone was built."

The next Norseman of note to sail up the river to London Bridge was Canute. He knew, of course, the perils of trying conclusions with the Londoners' bridge. Nor did he pit himself against London's massive and well-manned wall. No, Canute thought of a scheme for *by-passing* the bridge and making a landing farther upstream. Regarding this scheme, various authorities tell of the channel he dug from somewhere near Rotherhithe and Bermondsey, which went inland a little way and emerged again into the Thames where Battersea now stands, the eventuality of which was that he landed and became master of a considerable part of a country of which he later became king – and a good king, too, by the way.

There are various accounts of Canute's ditch-digging. One writer describes it as a colossal undertaking performed with great speed. But the odds seem against this guess at history, and a more accepted story is suggested by a writer in Knight's *London*. Canute in all likelihood, he says, found the new passage he wanted for his ships created by the natural inundation of the river, and only followed the guidance of the deeper and more navigable parts of the great marsh which then extended all along the south bank of the Thames in that part of its course. There was probably very little digging.

Soon after Canute had overrun much of England, especially in the north, King Ethelred died, to be succeeded by his son Edmund Ironside, who was already at war with Canute in

---

* For a note about Stow's life, see the Miscellany at the end of the book

various parts of the country. Later he and Canute came to terms on what might be termed a fifty-fifty basis over the territories each should rule. Shortly after this arrangement was made, Edmund met with an untimely end not, as has been suggested, at the instigation of Canute, who, however, became king of the whole of England. Thus Canute was king of this country and also of Denmark, Norway and Sweden.

He proved to be an exemplary ruler and, sending his Danish followers back to Denmark, set about restoring law and order in this country which had sadly lapsed under the rule of the not unsuitably named Ethelred the Unready.

London Bridge had no more to fear from the Norsemen.

The upkeep of the timber bridge was considerable largely because of the vicissitudes which attended it, and money had to be obtained from various sources. In examining these sources we come upon an interesting fact which appertains to this day. It appears from a charter of Henry I, in the year 1122, that a grant was made to the monks of Bermondsey Abbey of five shillings a year, which was a bigger sum than one might think. This grant was to be provided out of the lands pertaining to London Bridge. This is regarded as a beginning of these endowments of landed properties now forming the Bridge House Estates of today, an extremely wealthy body.

How much of the foregoing early history is legend we cannot with certainty say. I have quoted from writers of centuries ago who themselves delved back for even more centuries. Even old Stow occasionally found himself rummaging in the mists of far-off history, as he may have done before he came upon the report of Bartholomew Linstead, the last prior of St Mary Overie at Southwark, which helped him in his description of the foundation of the first London Bridge. In Knight's *London* (1851), in an article about the early London Bridge, the writer shines a comforting beam on those who have been baffled by the inconsistencies of the pre-Conquest history of England when minor details are involved. A quotation from his observations may well end this chapter:

"The legend (retailed by Stow) has acquired a prescriptive right to a place in any account of London Bridge, and pity it were that other of Whittington and his cat, should be discarded from the page of history merely as not an absolutely literal record of the fact; such touches or flourishes in the inventive line are part of that privilege of antiquity of which Livy has spoken in his genial way. . . . We have here, if not a true narrative, at least a true picture, which is quite as good; no rich old Southwark ferryman may have actually had an only daughter to inherit his wealth – no religious house, either of sisters or priests, may ever have risen out of the profits of any ferry across this part of the Thames – no such house may have had anything to do with the building of the first London Bridge; – but still in fiction, if such it be, is all true to the spirit of the time and the state of society in which it is laid, and carries us back just as effectually as if old Prior Linstead had been in a condition to make his affidavit to every word of it. It must be admitted, however, that to persons who care only about matters of fact, this report of the worthy Prior's cannot be very conscientiously recommended."

1. An ancient print of Southwark (foreground) with old London Bridge reaching to the City. The buildings on the left are places of amusement.

2. Eastern side of Southwark gate and tower, showing iron palings guarding the open spaces between the buildings.

3. London Bridge and the City sky-line beyond, c. 1620.

4. This panoramic view of Southwark and the City shows St Paul's Cathedral after lightning had destroyed its tall spire, but before the Great Fire of 1666 completely laid it low.

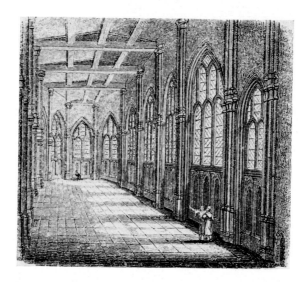

5. Interior view of the upper chapel in the Chapel of St Thomas, built on the centre pier of the stone bridge, 1209.

6. Harvard Chapel in Southwark Cathedral, sponsored by ex-Harvard students in memory of the Southwark-born founder of the American university.

7. Heads of the executed affixed on the Southwark gate of London Bridge.

8 and 9. Views of London Bridge from the east, after the buildings on it were demolished. St Paul's appears on the left of each picture, and the Monument on the right. Fierce currents pour through the arches at low tide (below).

10. The temporary bridge, built during the removal of houses from the old bridge, was mysteriously burned down in 1758.

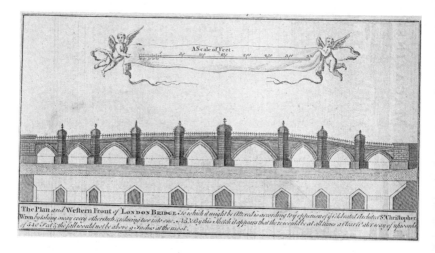

The Plan *and* Western Front *of* LONDON BRIDGE. *So which it might be altered is according to ý opinion of ý celebrated Architect* St Christopher Wren *by taking away every other arch, & placing two into one. & By this sketch it appears that there would be at all times a clear water way of upwards of 540 Feet, & the fall would not be above 9 Inches at the most.*

11. An idea of Christopher Wren's for reducing the number of arches and improving the flow of water under the old London Bridge.

12. The first iron bridge in the world, erected over the Severn in Shropshire in 1779. Plans for a single-span iron bridge for the new London Bridge were considered – but rejected.

3

THE FIRST STONE
BRIDGE

As we have seen, Peter de Colechurch was responsible for the last of the timber bridges, i.e. the last of a succession of re-buildings on the actual site of the original bridge, so often damaged or destroyed. It had become clear that the maintaining of a timber bridge was now a responsibility beyond the resources at hand, so perpetual were the needs of restoring it. Therefore the idea was mooted that there should be built a stone bridge more capable of standing up to the caprice of the elements.

Thus in 1176 Peter de Colechurch came into the picture again. There is little known about this priest-architect, except that he was a remarkable fellow, capable of mingling his work as a man of God with the more mundane occupation of building bridges, the first occupation on the north side of the river and the second on the south. It would have been interesting to have known just what manner of man he was. When the buildings on his stone bridge were demolished some six centuries later, and with them the chapel of St Thomas à Becket, where Peter was buried, his skeleton was found, but you cannot deduce much from a skeleton, certainly not from a six-centuries old one.

When Peter decided to embark on the new stone bridge he had to cast a calculating eye on where the money was coming from, as any good architect should. He was no doubt relieved to find that King Henry II was helpful in a somewhat unique manner. Henry imposed a tax on wool, the proceeds of which were to be devoted to the new London Bridge. This gave rise to the popular joke that "London Bridge was built on woolpacks". It was a somewhat wry joke, for it was the people who were paying, not the king. The tax, we read, was "upon all wools, wool-fells [that is the undressed sheepskins] and leather to be taken of the English as of strangers. . . . This amounted to half a mark [6s. 8d.] for every sack of wool of 26 stone weight; and a whole mark upon every last of leather."

The new stone bridge was built a little to the west of the existing timber bridge, and very close to it. Details of how Peter de Colechurch built it are scant and, in any case, too technical to be included here. It took thirty-three years to build, but Peter had been dead four years before the end of that period. Before his death he had been ailing for several years during which work on the bridge had been partly in abeyance, and it was not until the reign of King John that it was put into other hands. This appears a long delay, but it must be remembered that the reign between Henry II and John – that of Richard I (Coeur-de-Lion) lasted but ten years.

The news of his replacement had to be broken to Peter de Colechurch, and he is supposed to have taken it with perhaps grateful resignation. The truth is that King John himself was becoming impatient at the slow growth of the bridge, despite the fact that the old timber bridge was still holding good. There is no questioning the responsibility of King John himself for the change, since there is extant a letter from him to the mayor and citizens of London. It is in Latin and reposes in the Harleian MSS in the British Museum. Here is a translation of part of it:

"John, by the Grace of God King of England, etc. to his faithful and beloved the Mayor and Citizens of London, greeting. Considering how the Lord in a short time hath wrought in regard to the Bridges of Xainctes and Rochelle, by the great care and pains of our faithful, learned and worthy Clerk, Isenbert, Master of the Schools of Xainctes: We therefore by the advice of our Reverend Father in Christ, Hubert (Walter), Archbishop of Canterbury, and that of others, have desired, directed and enjoined him to use his best endeavour in building your bridge, for your benefit, and that of the public: For we trust in the Lord, that this Bridge, so requisite for you, and all who shall pass the same, will, through his industry and the divine blessing, soon be finished. Wherefore, without prejudice to our right, or that of the City of London, we will and grant, that the rents and profits of the several houses which the said Master of Schools shall cause to be erected on the Bridge aforesaid, be for ever appropriated to repair, maintain and uphold the same.

"And seeing that the requisite work of the Bridge cannot be accomplished without your aid, and that of others, we charge and exhort you, kindly to receive and honour the above-named Isenbert, and those employed by him, who will perform everything to your advantage and credit, according to his directions, you affording him your joint advice and assistance in the premises. For whatever good office or honour you shall do to him, you ought to esteem the same as done to Us. . . . But, should any injury be offered to the said Isenbert, or to the persons employed by him, which we do not believe there will, see that the same be redressed as soon as it comes to your knowledge.

"Witness myself, at Molinel in the Province of Bourbon, France, – the eighteenth day of April."

This letter is commended to the reader as a brief but re-deeming side-light on King John, who is generally regarded as the worst king who ever occupied the English throne. He was a king who did little right and multitudes of wrong. He fell foul of the Barons – to his cost at Runnymeade – he quarrelled with France and lost Normandy and, perhaps worst of all, murdered his young brother, Prince Arthur, who was the fourth son of their father, Henry II, while John himself was the fifth, with a lesser claim to the throne; and, overall, he was responsible for the national humiliation associated with his reign.

We must also give John credit for various financial notions concerning the building and upkeep of the new stone bridge. Thus, he obliged the City of London to use certain "void places" which he himself gave, to be put to profit by "building upon" and such profits thereof to remain towards the building and repairing of the same bridge.

We are not sure that King John's instructions regarding Isenbert were fully carried out, for we hear very little about him. Indeed, only a few years after John's letter to the mayor we read in Stow and elsewhere that the bridge was finished by the worthy merchants of London, Serle Mercer, William Almaine and Benedict Botewrite, "principal masters of that work". Of course we cannot always be one hundred per cent sure of any old historian's statement, and more than one antiquary has doubted Stow's contention that "the course of the river was, for the time, [i.e. during the building of the bridge] turned the other way about, by a trench cut for that purpose, beginning, as is supposed, east about Redriffe [Rotherhithe] and ending in the west about Patricksea, now termed Battersey".

This sounds as though Stow has allowed Canute's canal, about which we have read earlier, to seep into his mind. Historian Maitland, however, considers "from an actual inspection of the piers of the bridge, that it had evidently been raised on strong frames of piles driven into the bed of the river, as might very easily have been done without the water having been withdrawn, the first layer of stones being in this way only about three feet below the low-water mark".

Be all this as it may, the bridge in due course was erected, of considerable beauty and astonishing strength.

The numerous houses and other buildings erected on Peter de Colechurch's bridge contributed, naturally, to the upkeep of the structure by way of rents. It may not be amiss here to mention a few plain facts about this bridge. It consisted of twenty stone arches of irregular construction and of various sizes, the centre arch being 72 feet in width, and the others varying from 8 feet to 20 feet. The height in the centre was 60 feet, and the total length 915 feet. The carriage-way was a comfortable 31 feet broad, and the footway on each side 7 feet. The space between the piers, being contracted by the size of the "starlings" or "sterlings" occasioned a rise and fall of four or five feet with the ebb and flow of each tide, so that it was unsafe for any reasonably sized boat to pass through except at high-water. The "sterlings" referred to were large, boat-shaped supports of masonry around each pier, and may easily be seen in plates 3 and 4. From these it is obvious that when the water level was below the sterlings, the river's mass of water had to pour through narrower channel space, a constriction which naturally increased the velocity of the current (plate 9).

In consequence of this, it was a dangerous matter to "shoot the arches" and there were regular fatal accidents. It was even dangerous when the water was a foot or two above the sterlings so that barges might "run aground" and either capsize or have to stay there in the hope that the next high tide would lift them off.

The bridge had a gate-house at each end and a drawbridge in the middle. This drawbridge was a great source of revenue to the bridge in its earlier days, in as much as a toll of twelve pence was imposed on all ships passing under the bridge when the drawbridge was raised for their accommodation. Twelve pence was a considerable sum in those days.

Two other features of the bridge were the chapel of Thomas à Becket and the strange, magnificent edifice called Nonsuch House. We will take a look at these two remarkable features presently. Meanwhile, to further our appreciation of Cole-church's bridge in retrospect, it is apt to quote the words of that superb antiquarian John Timbs in his *Curiosities of London*, a large, closely type-set book of nearly a thousand pages.

"The chronicles of this stone bridge [he says] through nearly six centuries and a quarter form, perhaps, the most interesting episode in the history of London. The scenes of fire and siege, insurrection and popular vengeance, of national rejoicing and of the pageant victories of man and of death, of fame or funeral – it were impossible for us to attempt to recite. . . . In 1212 [he continues] within four years after the bridge being finished, there was a terrible conflagration at each end, when nearly 3,000 persons perished; in 1264, Henry III was repulsed here by de Montfort, earl of Leicester, and the populace attacked the queen in her barge as it was preparing to shoot the bridge; in 1381, the rebel Wat Tyler entered the City by this road; in 1392 Richard II was received here in great pomp by the citizens; in 1415 it was the scene of a grand triumph by Henry V, and in 1422 of his funeral procession; in 1428 the duke of Norfolk's barge was lost by upsetting at the bridge, and His Grace narrowly escaped; in 1450 –

> *Jack Cade hath gotten London Bridge; the citizens*
> *Fly and forsake their houses*

but the rebel was defeated, and his head placed upon the gate-house; in 1477 Falconbridge (known as the Bastard) attacked the bridge and fired several houses; in 1545 it was one of the daring scenes of Sir Thomas Wyatt's rebellion; in 1632 more than one third of the houses were consumed in an accidental conflagration; and in 1666 part of the labyrinth of houses was swept away by the Great Fire; the whole street was rebuilt within twenty years; but in 1757 the houses were entirely removed, and parapets and balustrades erected on each side; in this state the bridge remained till its demolition.''

Timbs could have mentioned many other exciting happenings which brightened up Colechurch's bridge, but he has not done too badly! As we shall presently be reviewing them a little more closely and perhaps dealing with a few omissions, we will leave it at that.

We may now take a look at the variety of buildings on the bridge with their inhabitants and purposes at that time. As to the buildings, our illustrations provide a clear idea of them, though pictures are but poor compensation for recent generations never having seen them. Lucky the citizens who saw, as a near everyday sight, the morning sun from downriver, which is eastwards, catching the miscellany of buildings which huddled along the length of Peter de Colechurch's London Bridge. It must be remembered that the buildings were not begun to be removed until 1757 and that there were already many good artists at work who left us exquisite pictures in oils and water-colour. A number of these were, in 1968, on view in a remarkable exhibition in the Guildhall Art Gallery, called "London Bridge in Art". Some of these may still be seen on application at Guildhall.

Just how many houses stood on London Bridge I cannot venture to say; accounts differ so widely. Or maybe the number of houses varied from time to time in the more than six hundred years of its existence. This would be understandable when its various vicissitudes are considered, such as the fires which burnt down houses wholesale, many of which perhaps were not rebuilt for indefinite periods. We know, however, that the houses and other buildings lined the bridge on both sides. The same discrepancies occur in the differing accounts of the width of the "street" – for street it was. In one account we are told that there was a footpath on either side along which pedestrians could cross the bridge in safety; in another the difficulty of crossing the bridge on foot is told as a tale of horror. Even Norden, who wrote in Elizabeth's day, stated that the bridge was "adorned with sumptuous buildings and statelie and beautiful houses on either side", but he seemed unaware of any footpaths, and he went on to say that the bridge was one continuous street "except certain void places for the retyre of passengers from the danger of cars, carts and droves of cattle usually passing that way", through which vacancies only could the river be seen over the parapet walls and palings (plate 2).

A writer in Knight's *London* seems to have had a little difficulty with his facts, for he states of the bridge "at the widest parts the 'street' was no more than twenty feet broad, and in some places it narrowed to twelve; so we may conceive what a scene of confusion and pass of peril it must have been, without footways, and with a torrent of carts, coaches and other vehicles constantly pouring along in both directions – unless when matters were made still worse by two crossing wagons, more highly loaded than usual, being caught between the projecting first floors, to the stoppage of the whole accumulating mass of traffic in the rear of each, and the entire blocking of the passage. The common and the only tolerably safe plan for the pedestrian adventurer who sought to make his way through the tumult, was to get into the wake of some carriage, and keep close to it at whatever rate it might be going, till he was fairly across the bridge, or had reached his point of destination."

The above is strange reading, but it may be of some oblique satisfaction to the "pedestrian adventurer" of this day!

Apart from the houses of varying distinction, the chief buildings are the Chapel of Thomas à Becket, Nonsuch House and the gatehouses at each end which were tower-like in shape, and which at one time were surmounted by the poles bearing the heads of traitors.

The Chapel of Thomas à Becket was so named by Peter de Colechurch because at his church in Poultry Becket was baptised. Considering its position it was an extraordinarily large and heavy structure, projecting well over the level of the parapet of the bridge, and reaching down to the sterling at the base of one of the piers which supported the building. In all it was some forty feet in height, and dominated the river above and below it. From some angles it appeared octagonal in shape, with pinnacles adorning its roof. Its main window was gothic and of great beauty. It had various chapels and was well maintained with priests. It also had a crypt within a pier of the bridge, and it was here that the tomb of Peter de Cole-church was found at the demolition of the chapel. Long before this, most of the chapel had been converted into dwelling-places.

Fig. 2. A sketch of the St Thomas à Becket Chapel which stood on London Bridge, after its conversion into a dwelling-house and warehouse.

Nonsuch House was a unique construction which stood a little to the City side of the chapel. It had been made of wood in Holland and transported piecemeal to the Thames. Its erection called for no bricks or morter, the whole being fitted together by means of wooden pegs without the help of so much as a nail. It extended across the bridge by means of an archway, a fantastic building which delighted the eyes of the citizens. Briefly, in Knight's words,

". . . it was elaborately carved both on its principal front towards Southwark, and on its east and west gables, which protruded a considerable way beyond the line of the bridge, while the square towers at each of its four corners, crowned by

Fig. 3. Nonsuch House on London Bridge, seen from the south-west. The blocks of wood from which it was constructed were imported piecemeal from Holland.

Kremlin spires, and their gilded vanes, were seen from all directions ascending above all the surrounding buildings."

Just how or why or by whom Nonsuch House was brought in such an eccentric manner from Holland to London Bridge is not easy to ascertain, but the citizens of London and Southwark apparently took it for granted. Eventually, like the Chapel of St Thomas à Becket, it was turned into tenements. The former, however, did stand intact and performed its religious functions until the Reformation and beyond.

Prior to the erection of Nonsuch House there had stood on its site near the drawbridge a solid watch-tower on which were posted an array of "traitors'" heads. This tower was taken down in 1577 and the heads removed to the tower at the

Southwark end of the bridge. These gruesome exhibits were familiar sights to Londoners. Indeed they were so much a part of the London Bridge scene that a short chapter is devoted to them later in our book. Many were the stories attached to them, as shall be seen.

Fig. 4. Nonsuch House from the west, showing the racing currents between the sterlings.

As we have noticed, many were the disasters which overtook Peter de Colechurch's stone bridge. The first tragedy to befall the bridge was a disastrous fire on the night of 10 July 1212. For many years after it, the bridge stood in a ruinous condition, but it was eventually restored to its former self. No sooner had this been accomplished than calamity again struck the bridge. There had been a long and severe frost, with snow-storms, in what we now call the Thames Valley, and, indeed, all the way down to London. Then came the thaw and the

river was soon carrying great masses of broken ice which crashed
into the piers and sterlings because of the swiftness of the
current between the narrow arches, with the result that five
of these arches were swept away altogether. Temporary structures were soon put up and in due course the bridge was itself
again. It is possible that the old timber bridge was at this time
able to deputise for the damaged new one, though it must have
been in a dilapidated condition.

The next catastrophe of note was in 1437 when "the great
stone gate at London Bridge, with the tower upon it, next to
Southwark, fell down, and two of the farthest arches of the
same bridge, and yet no man perished in body, which was a
great work of God".

Two more serious fires, not restricted to the bridge alone
but to larger areas of London, are a part of the history of the
first stone bridge. One occurred in 1633, and the other was the
Great Fire of London of 1666.

We hear little of the results of these disasters upon the
inhabitants of the houses on London Bridge. They were an
interesting collection, varying, of course, over the years. Their
occupations, however, did not seem to change much over the
centuries. Thus there were makers of pins and needles, and one
reads of ladies coming from as far afield as St James's to make
economical purchases of both. Even today the searcher after
curious objects on the muddy foreshore of the river at low
water may collect as many as a dozen old-fashioned, rusty pins
in a few hours. I have done so myself within a hundred yards
of London Bridge.

An early writer compiled a short list of the occupations
pursued on the bridge. It includes six hosiers, five haberdashers
of hats, one shoemaker, two glovers, one girdler, one "distiller
of strong waters", and two grocers. Added to these are one
scrivener, one curate of St Magnus' church, and a clerk of the
same. But the most common occupation seems to have been
publishing and book-selling. Indeed the bridge almost ranked
with Paternoster Row and St Paul's Churchyard in this
respect. We have read in an earlier chapter of the odd pamphlet
about the eccentric ferryman, published at the sign of the
Looking Glass on London Bridge. Other publishers' signs were
the Three Bibles, the Angel and the Black Boy. Most of these

signs, like similar ones scattered all over London, above shops, inns and private houses, were of considerable weight and were hung on projecting brackets above the respective doors. They swung in the wind, creaking violently as they did so. Occasionally one would fall, bringing death or injury to pedestrians below. Eventually these signs were forbidden in certain parts of London, unless they were fixed flush with the wall of the building. Many of them were invested with a romantic origin not always justified, especially when the sign disappeared and its name was carried on by the immediate locality. Thus, even today, there is a narrow passage running out of and parallel to Whitefriars Street off Fleet Street, bearing the name of Hanging Sword Alley. This has acquired many sinister implications, whereas its origin was the private sign of a merchant who had his house there. Nevertheless, perhaps the sinister application was not unjustified, since it was once called Bloodbowl Alley on account of a house there which had been the scene of more than one sanguinary murder.

Various artists found dwelling on London Bridge to their liking. The foremost of these was the German Hans Holbein who, after several lengthy visits to England, took up permanent dwelling here, having become principal painter to Henry VIII. Horace Walpole, the famous author and gossip of the eighteenth century, tells us that "the father of the Lord Treasurer of Oxford, passing over London Bridge was caught in a shower; and, stepping into a goldsmiths shop for shelter, found there a picture by Holbein who had lived in that house. He offered the goldsmith £100 for it, who consented to let him have it, but desired first to show it to some persons. Immediately after occurred the Great Fire of London, and the picture was destroyed." This suggests that Holbein lived on the City end of the bridge, which was the part affected by the fire. A modern book of reference states that Holbein lived in the parish of St Andrew Undershaft (Stow's church) which suggests that some of the bridge houses belonged to this parish in Eastcheap, which is quite near the bridge, though St Magnus the Martyr is more likely, being nearer still.

Another artist who chose to live on London Bridge was the marine painter, Peter Monamy, who received his early tuition in painting from a sign-painter on London Bridge. Of him it was said that "the shallow waves that rolled under his window fitted him to paint the turbulence of the ocean". This quotation, like the one above, comes from the loquacious Horace Walpole. William Hogarth, too, is reputed to have lived on the bridge for a period, but this idea seems to have been born of his series

Fig. 5. Hogarth's portrayal of old houses on London Bridge.

of engravings "Marriage à la Mode", one of which portrays faithfully the houses on the bridge.

Many other great characters of the past are reputed in various works to have lived on London Bridge, including John Bunyan, but the evidence is generally too slender to warrant recognition here.

4

HEADS ON THE BRIDGE

It is a curious thought that the earlier period of the civilised stone bridge, with its priest-architect, its neighbouring monkish establishments, its numerous churches named after saints, its celebrated artists and poets, and its refinements in high places, should have continuously been guilty of barbarisms unknown before or after that period. Thus, it was not sufficient to sentence a man to death and hang him, but, in addition, to inflict *post mortem* indignities almost unmentionable on his body. This applied mainly to the higher ranks of those executed. Highwaymen and thieves were hanged and suspended in chains from various gallows, but their heads were generally allowed to remain on their bodies. Not so in the case of their betters, whose heads were frequently cut off, placed on poles and exhibited in public places, notably on the tower at the Southwark end of London Bridge – sometimes as many as twelve to twenty in rotting, grisly groups (plate 7). These were generally the heads of so-called traitors, high-born "rebels" against the Church or the state.

One of the early heads to be set up on London Bridge was that of Sir William Wallace, the past, present and future hero of Scotland. The circumstances of its appearance there are worth recording. King Edward I of England was continuously trying to subdue the Scots who, on their side, loathed the English, partly because the English soldiery maltreated the Scots whenever they had the chance. Wallace, whose history is somewhat obscure, mustered a Scottish army to withstand the persecution of his country by Edward. He attacked the English court of justice at Scone, and generally showed that the Scots were not to be trifled with. Edward sent a large force into Scotland, but it was nearly wiped out by Wallace at Stirling. Eventually Edward, who had been abroad, returned to England

and led a much greater force into Scotland. Wallace's army had been considerably strengthened since Stirling, by hosts of admirers, but Edward inflicted a severe reverse on the Scots at Falkirk. The Wallace army disintegrated and Wallace fled into hiding, probably among the Scottish mountains; but he was betrayed by ill-wishers, was captured and taken to London in chains. He was a man of great strength and noble in appearance, so that when he was paraded through London to the Tower, on a led horse, with courage gleaming in his eye, not a few of the onlookers were in sympathy with him.

But he was taken to Westminster Hall, tried and sentenced to be executed as a traitor. Courageous to the last, he told the tribunal that he could not be a traitor to Edward of England, "for he never was my king".

Here comes the shocking part of the story. After his execution his body was taken down and his head severed to be taken to London Bridge and set upon a pole. But there was worse to come; his body was "quartered" and the four pieces sent to Scotland, there to be exhibited in four different parts of the country, "as a lesson to others". One writer, going into details which we shall not repeat here, states that the four quarters of Wallace's body, before they left London, were enclosed in four leaden caskets, "for keeping". All this was done at the orders of Edward I himself. Prior to this, runs a narrative, "this man of Belial [Wallace!] after innumerable crimes, was taken by the King's officers, and, *by his command*, brought up to be judged by himself, attended by the Nobles of the Kingdom of England, on the vigil of St Bartholomew's Day – the 23rd of August – where he was condemned to a most cruel, but unworthy death," though firstly he was dragged at the tail of a horse through the fields of London to a very high gibbet, upon which he was hung with a halter.

Nevertheless, none of this prevented Wallace becoming a hero to his people. Long afterwards a poem of 5,000 couplets was written by the famous poet and reciter, Blind Harry, otherwise Henry the Minstrel. But no poem has outlasted that of Robert Burns' "Scots wha hae wi' Wallace bled".

There was a repetition of this "distribution of quarters" in the case of an early Bolingbroke who was hanged at Tyburn, having been dragged from the Tower. His head was posted on

London Bridge and the four sections of his body sent to Hereford, Oxford, Cambridge and York. The common folk thought this added distinction to him, which was not what his betters intended. Another victim of the times was the duke of Northumberland, later earl of Warwick, of the family of Percy, a member of which was the celebrated Hotspur. He was a great soldier and administrator but this did not count against his political activities. Treason, they were called.

The stories of the heads on London Bridge are many and dismal and might well cease here, but there are two which cannot possibly be omitted from our account. They are those of John Fisher, a distinguished prelate, and his friend Sir Thomas More, who were executed for their refusal to acknowledge Henry VIII as the supreme head of the Church. They were far from being the only ones to suffer for the same reason, but they are the only two whose heads made history on London Bridge. True it is that superstition and legend enter into their stories, but they are fascinating stories, nevertheless.

Fisher, after a distinguished academic career at Cambridge, became bishop of Rochester, and might well have remained so but for his opposition to Henry VIII's divorce from Catherine of Aragon and his refusal to acknowledge Henry as head of the Church. He was executed on Tower Hill in 1535. It is interesting to note that in 1935, the 400th anniversary of his death, he was canonised as St John of Rochester. His festival is 22 June, the anniversary of his execution.

At about the time of his imprisonment Fisher received a cardinal's hat from Rome. Said Henry VIII: "Let the Pope send him a hat if he wishes. Mother of God, he shall wear it on his shoulders, for I will leave him never a head to put it on." And so it was; his head was duly set upon a pole on London Bridge, though there was a little delay about this owing to Henry's wish to show the head to Anne Boleyn, the successor to Queen Catherine of Aragon. A pretty touch, as one might say.

But, according to the story, it seemed that Fisher's head came near to having the last word in the matter. I quote from an account given by historian Hall, to whom many writers on old London owe a debt. (Hall was a Shropshire man who lived at the end of the fifteenth century. He represented a Shropshire division in Parliament and at the same time held several high positions in the City of London. Shakespeare, it is said, relied on him for many historical facts. He was said to be "a Protestant, a Royalist, a hater of priests and a lover of pageants".)

"The next day after his burying, the head, after being parboyled, was pricked upon a pole and set high upon London Bridge, among the rest of the holy Carthusians' heads that suffered death lately before him. And here I cannot omit to declare unto you the miraculous sight of this head which, after it had stood up the space of fourteen days on London Bridge, could not be perceived to waste or consume, neither for the weather, which was then very hot, neither for the parboyling in hot water, but grew daily fresher and fresher, so that in his lifetime he never looked so well; for, his cheeks being beautified with a comely red, the face looked as though it had beholden the people passing by, and would have spoken to them, which many took for a miracle, that Almighty God was pleased to show against the course of Nature, in this preserving the fresh and lively colour of his face, surpassing the colour he had when alive, whereby was noted to the world the innocence and holiness of the beloved father, that thus innocently was content to lose his head in defence of his Mother, the Holy Catholique Church of Christ.

"Wherefore the people coming daily to see this strange sight, the passage over the Bridge was so stopped with their coming and going, that neither cart nor horse could pass, and therefore, at the end of fourteen days, the executioner was commanded to throw downe the head into the River of Thames, and, in place thereof, was set the head of the most blessed and constant martyr, Sir Thomas More, his companion, and fellow in all his troubles, who suffered his passion the 6th July next following, about nine o'clock in the morning."

If the authorities thought this juggling with heads was going to detract from the miracle of Fisher, they were mistaken, for Sir Thomas More's head was equally "obstinate" and refused to show any signs of wear and tear. According to an account of Sir Thomas's grandson, who wrote his biography, "after the head had been exposed for some months, being about to be cast into the Thames, because room should be made for divers others, who, in plentiful sort, suffered martyrdom for the same supremacy", More's head was bought by his daughter Margaret, when it was found to be in a miraculous state of preservation. "The hairs of his head, being almost grey before his martyrdom, they seemed now to be as it were reddish or yellow."

The execution of Sir Thomas More shows Henry VIII at his most callous and senseless. Granted that More refused to acknowledge the king as head of the Church, he was yet one of the great Englishmen of the day, an asset to his country's culture, to its legislature and to the upkeep of its honour at home and abroad. At one time Henry held him in high favour. He was Speaker to the House of Commons, and ultimately Lord Chancellor; he was also the author of that remarkable and ever remembered book *Utopia*, whose title gave a new and permanent epithet to the English language. Yet Henry had him branded as a traitor and treated as we have seen.

His daughter Margaret is said to have preserved his head in a leaden casket and to have had it buried with her in a vault under a chapel at St Dunstan's, Canterbury.

The catalogue of innocent heads that shamed London Bridge could be only with difficulty compiled, ranging as it did from the protestant dictates of Henry VIII – with the boy king Edward VI's brief reign under regencies – to the violent persecutions of Catholic Mary Tudor who, in the last few years of her reign, wiped out a good slice of the religious intelligentsia of England. But the catalogue would go further back than that. For instance there was the melancholy episode of Simon Frisel who was taken prisoner from the Scots by Edward I a year after the capture of Wallace. Here is an account of his treatment as culled from an old poem describing the event:

"With fetters and leg-irons he was drawn from the Tower of London, dressed in a short coat of coarse cloth, through Cheapside, having on his head a garland of the last fashion; and many Englishmen, to see Simon Frisel, ran thither. Then was he brought to the gibbet, and first being hung, he was also beheaded, which he thought it long to be endured. After he was opened and his bowels burned; but his head was sent to London Bridge to affright the beholders; so ever might I thrive, as that once he little thought to stand there."

This "translation" of the old poem has been described as written on old discoloured parchment, in a square gothic text, the ink of which is turned brown by time, with many contractions, and vile spelling.

The supremacy of Henry VIII over the Church or, rather, the luckless ones who denied it and were found out, was responsible for scores of heads appearing on London Bridge, for the Act decreeing the latter as Treason was wide in its scope and included both clergy and laymen. At one single instance of time a German statesman visiting England, a Herr Hentzner, counted the heads on the Southwark Gate and recorded them as over thirty.

Wallace's head was not the first to have the honour (if honour it were) of being stuck up on London Bridge. That belonged to the head of the Carthusian prior, John Houghton. This was followed by the heads of a number of lesser monks of the Carthusian Charterhouse over which Prior Houghton presided. (The name Charterhouse had its significance at the time, for the Carthusian Order was founded by St Bruno at Chartreuse in France, and so a Carthusian monastery in England was called a Charterhouse.)

With the exit of the soul of Bluff King Hal, to somewhere or other, the number of heads on the bridge decreased, and when the "exhibition" was moved to Temple Bar they were fewer still. It is worth noting, however, that with the Restoration, a few of the regicides' heads stood above the swirling Thames.

Speaking of the heads on Temple Bar, that inveterate letter-writer, *litterateur* and gossip, Horace Walpole, wrote that many idle youths did very well at Temple Bar by loaning small telescopes to bystanders wishing for a closer look – at a halfpenny a time. Whether the Southwark youths were so enterprising is not told.

In the reign preceding Henry VIII's – that of Henry VII – there occurred a rebellion which, though not widely mentioned in our histories, might nevertheless have been a serious matter for London Bridge and, indeed, for the City itself. For want of a better name we shall call it the Cornish Rebellion. It began as a result of "a subsidy voted by Parliament in 1496", though what that subsidy was is not easily ascertained. The prime movers were Thomas Flamoke, a lawyer, and a Bodmin blacksmith named Joseph. At the time of the disturbance Henry VII with a small army was marching to Scotland, nominally at war. At the news that the Cornish rebels were marching towards London in strength, the forces were turned back to deal with the matter.

Meanwhile the rebels reached Blackheath where they were strongly opposed by the king's men, whereupon a number of the rebels, not liking the look of things, deserted the main body. This was just as well for them, for in a short battle, the rebels were routed and both Flamoke and blacksmith Joseph – though called by Stow "men of good stomackes" – were captured. A week later both were hanged at Tyburn, and it was intended that their quartered bodies should be sent for erection in different parts of Cornwall. But, according to Hall, the Shropshire historian, it was feared that the Cornishmen would start more trouble in retaliation, so the bodies were dealt with on the spot, and the heads placed on London Bridge. Some accounts say that the quartered corpses were placed there too.

It was rare for four important political heads to be erected on London Bridge at the same time, which was what happened after the dethronement of the still youthful Richard II *circa* 1400. He was imprisoned in the Tower, after his successor-to-be, Henry of Lancaster, made certain charges against him. Henry also seized four nobles who had been Richard's favourites and who had been implicated in certain murders, including that of Richard's uncle, the duke of Gloucester. The nobles were Sir Bernard Brocas, Lord Marclais, Master John Derby, Receiver of Lincoln, and Lord Stelle, Steward of the King's Household, all of them known to be opposers of Henry's accession as Henry IV.

The most authentic account of the matter is that of Jean Froissart, the eminent contemporary French chronicler. Here is a translation of his description:

"They were tried before the Lord Mayor and others at Guildhall, and were sentenced to be brought before the apartment of the Tower of London in which King Richard was confined, that he might see from his windows, and there drawn on sledges by horses to Cheapside, each person separately, and there beheaded, their heads affixed to spikes on London Bridge, and their bodies hung upon a gibbet, and there left. Everything being prepared, the Mayor of London, and the lords who had assisted him in his judgment, set out from Guildhall with a large body of people, and came to the Tower of London, where they seized the four Knights of the King. They were all brought into the court[yard] and each tied to two horses, in the sight of all in the Tower, who were eye-witnesses of it as well as the King, who was much displeased, and in despair; for the remainder of the King's Knights who were with him looked for similar treatment, so cruel and revengeful did they know the Londoners. Without saying a word, these four were dragged through the streets to Cheapside, and on a fishmonger's stall had their heads struck off, which were placed over the gate of London Bridge, and their bodies hung on a gibbet. After this execution, every man retired to his home."

Richard II was sent to Pontefract Castle where he died or was murdered at the age of thirty-three. It should be noted that this was the Richard who, as a mere boy, faced Wat Tyler and his rebel rout, as described in our chapter "Rebels at the Gate".

A sad little story crops up from 1642 relating to a priest of the order of St Francis, named Henry Heath, who, for reasons we are not told, came to England from Douai. Apparently, owing to his extreme poverty, he made his way on foot to London. His story is told by Bishop Challoner in his book on Catholic martyrs.

"At London he arrives weary, as well he might, having travelled barefoot forty miles that day, and it being the winter season. It is now time to take up his quarters and give some little rest and refreshment to the body. But how shall this be done, for money he has none, nor acquaintances? However, he ventures to call at the Star Inn, near London Bridge, but the people at the house, finding that he has no money, turn him out of doors at eight o'clock on a cold winter night."

Next he laid himself down at a citizen's door and was taken up as a would-be shop-lifter. He was searched and upon him were some papers which showed that he was a Roman Catholic priest, to which he confessed. That was enough. He was tried under an existing statute and executed at Tyburn, his head afterwards being erected on London Bridge.

My last story in this somewhat macabre chapter has its amusing side. In the reign of Elizabeth our coinage had become debased to some extent and was ordered to be delivered to the Tower, there to be dealt with by German and Dutch workmen who had some experience of metals, also of the fumes of arsenic and sulphur which would arise from the melting of such metals. So far, so good; but the fumes proved too much for the workmen who, to a man, fell seriously ill. Some quack or other apparently came upon the scene, and, running true to certain superstitions of the age, advised drinking from a dead man's skull as an antidote. Accordingly, those in charge of the work obtained a warrant from "the Counsaile" to take down certain heads from the bridge for this excellent object, from which cups were made. An authority tells us that many of the men "dranke and founde some reliefe, although moost of them dyed".

5

━━∽∘◉∘⋴━━

SCENES OF POMP
AND POWER

Old London Bridge in its centuries of service provided Londoners with a succession of excitements, ranging from sanguinary struggles against rebel armies to peace-time pageantry on the grand scale. The former are dealt with later in the chapter called "Rebels at the Gate", while in the present chapter we take a look at the fantastic happenings which must have provided those early citizens with many a talking point. News, when they received any, had come through many tortuous channels, tinctured and embellished on its way, but the happenings on London Bridge were for all to see and appraise. It would have been interesting to have heard the comments of the thousands of onlookers on one of the most colourful of all pageants which crossed the bridge when Cardinal Wolsey set off to France on a mission concerned with the matrimonial affairs of Henry VIII. His route was via the bridge, through Southwark and thence to the Dover Road and the coast.

Meanwhile it is worth taking a brief look at Wolsey, that indelible figure in English history, that son of an Ipswich butcher whose domination over English and European diplomacy scarcely knew any bounds for a period which was to end with dramatic suddenness at the hands of Henry VIII whom he had alike dominated.

Wolsey had left his native Ipswich and gone to Oxford where, academically, he conquered it, thence passing into the Church and the realm of high international politics. This was in the reign of Henry VII, and on the accession of Henry VIII in 1509 his influence rapidly grew and he soon gained the confidence of the new monarch. His power increased still further when he inflicted a diplomatic defeat on Ferdinand of Spain by forming an alliance with France. He achieved the eminence of cardinal and became Lord Chancellor. He also rose to great wealth, a fact which enabled him to build the astonishing Hampton Court Palace, an offset, perhaps, to his consciousness of a comparatively common upbringing. As mentioned in an earlier chapter, he later handed Hampton Court to the king in the face of jealousy on the part of those who resented the arrogance and power of "a low-born cardinal".

But royal favour in those days was fickle. Wolsey failed to compel the pope to countenance Henry's anulment of his marriage to Catherine of Aragon, a device to allow him to marry Anne Boleyn. Wolsey's high state collapsed. He had, as Shakespeare put it, swum on bubbles. Henry dismissed him from all his high offices except that of the archbishopric of York. A cynic might say that there was a catch even in that, for he was ordered to go there and remain in his diocese. This he did until he was summoned to London to face a strange charge of High Treason. This unhappy prospect, however, was dissolved when, breaking his long journey at Leicester, he died at the abbey there. Who knows that, but for this intervention of Providence, his head might not have grinned from the bridge over which, not many years before, had passed his great cavalcade which we now go on to describe?

There are various accounts of this occasion, but the best is by Cavendish in his biography, *The Life of Cardinal Wolsey*:

"Then marched he [Wolsey] forward out of his house at Westminster, passing all through London, over London Bridge, having before him of gentlemen a great number, three in a rank, in black velvet livery coats, and the most part of them with great gold chains about their necks. And all his yeomen, with noblemen's and gentlemen's servants following him in French tawny livery coats, having embroidered upon the backs and breasts of the said coats these letters: T. and C. under the Cardinal's hat. His sumpter mules, which were twenty in number or more, with his carts and other carriages of his train, were passed on before, conducted and guarded with a great number of bows and spears. He rode like a Cardinal, very sumtuously, on a mule trapped with crimson velvet upon velvet, and his stirrups of copper and gilt, and his spare mule following him with like apparel. And before him he had his two great crosses of silver, two great pillars of silver, the Great Seal of England, the Cardinal's Hat, and a gentleman that carried his valaunce, otherwise called a cloakbag, which was made altogether of fine scarlet cloth, embroidered over and over with cloth of gold very richly, having in it a cloak of fine scarlet. Thus passed he over London Bridge and all the way of his journey, having his harbingers passing before to provide lodging for his train."

King Richard II could not complain of a dull life, even after his confrontation of Wat Tyler and his hordes, which filled the citizens with pride that their boy king was possessed of so much courage. Richard's reign, including some ten years as a minor, lasted twenty-three years and ended with his murder (it is accepted) at Pontefract Castle in 1400. During the dozen or so adult years of his reign he taught the Londoners a good deal about royal pageantry where London Bridge was concerned. Indeed those years were marked by such kingly extravagance that the citizens, when asked by him for a loan of £1,000 – an immense sum in those days – demurred, though not whole-heartedly, for they still remembered the Wat Tyler episode.

Richard was incensed by their refusal and retaliated in a manner which surprised them. He summoned Parliament to meet him at Stamford in Lincolnshire and removed the Justiciary to York. Some say that this strong action of the king "brought the citizens to their senses", for their London had been bereft of much of its importance. Certainly reconciliation was not long in coming, though the most credible cause of it was the mediation of Richard's very worthy wife whom he had married some four years before as Anne of Bohemia. It was agreed between the citizens and Richard that he should re-enter the City with his queen in a grand procession from Windsor which he had made his personal headquarters. This procession "formed up" at Wandsworth and made a triumphal march, via Southwark, to London Bridge, which it crossed amid wild scenes of civic jubilation. At the gate of the bridge the king was presented with "two white fair steeds, trapped in gold, parted of red and white, hanged full with silver bells, the which present he thankfully received." (Another account says that the queen, also, was presented with a white palfrey similarly caparisoned.)

As to the cavalcade itself, the Londoners had rarely seen such a display. At Southwark the procession was met by the mayor, the bishop of London and "his clergy of the City", followed by five hundred boys in surplices. The *Chronicles of London Bridge* says:

"The other streets of London, too, put on all their bravery; the windows and walls being hung with cloths of gold, silver and silk; the Conduit in Cheapside poured out floods of red and white wine; a child, habited like an angel, crowned the King and Queen with golden crowns, from a sumptuous stage covered with performers in rich dresses; a table of the Trinity wrought in gold, and valued at £800 was given to the King, and another of St Anne to his consort. And truly I know of nothing which might so well express of that day as the passage with which Walsingham concludes his notice of it: 'There was so much glory,' says he, 'so much pomp, so great diversity of furniture provided, that to have undertaken it might have been a triumph for any King. For horses and trappings, plate of gold and silver, clothes of gold, silver, silk and velvet, ewers and basons of yellow gold, gold in coin, precious stones and jewels so rich, excellent and beautiful, were given to him, that their value and price might not easily be estimated'."

Two years after this hatchet-burying display, the good Queen Anne died of the plague at Sheen. In a short time she had shown herself to be one of the best consorts of any English king, and it is not being too imaginative to say that, had she lived, Richard's end might have been less unfortunate than it was.

Four years later Richard married the eight-year-old Isabella, daughter of Henry VI of France, having concluded a peace treaty with that feeble-minded monarch. This was to occasion a further example of pageantry. The marriage, performed by the archbishop of Canterbury, took place in Calais, where Richard spent fabulous sums on entertainment. The return route, when the royal party reached England, was by way of Southwark and London Bridge, where thousands had gathered to see the "little Queen". So great was the assembly on London Bridge that nine people were crushed to death, including the good prior of Tiptree in Essex. The procession which led the king and his young bride over the bridge included the mayor and aldermen of the City, "habited in scarlet", and many other colourful bodies.

For the next three years Richard ruled arbitrarily, and many cruel executions and banishments were of his doing. The end of his reign came quickly and he was forced to hand over the "ensigns of Royalty" to the duke of Lancaster who became Henry IV. Richard was put in the Tower, as we have seen, thence taken to Pontefract Castle and murdered – just how or by whom has never been truly discovered.

The next pageant we shall notice was staged on the return of King Henry V from his famous victory at Agincourt. The battle of Agincourt was destined to occupy an honoured place in English history until this day, and even the date – 1415 – is remembered by every schoolboy properly taught the history of his country. Briefly, at this battle, Henry V in person commanded the English army of about 9,000 men against the French 30,000 or more and defeated them, being wounded himself in this fiercest of conflicts. Only a few hundred British were killed, while the French losses were estimated at some 8,000, not to mention 1,000 prisoners whom Henry duly took back to England shortly after the battle. The king came to the City by the established route of Southwark and London Bridge.

The scene at London Bridge was a triumph of splendour and invention as may be gathered from the following extract from a contemporary account:

"On the top of the tower at the entrance to the Bridge . . . there stood on high a figure of gigantic magnitude, fearlessly looking in the King's face, as if he would do battle; but on his right and left hand were the great keys of the City hanging to a staff as though he had been gate-keeper. . . . And the towers about them were ornamented with halberts and the Royal Arms; and trumpeters stood aloft in the turrets, which were resounding with horns and clarions in winding and expanding melody . . . and there appeared on both sides all along the

Bridge very little youths. . . . And on the summit of the column on the right side, was the figure of an Antelope rampant, having a splendid figure of the Royal Arms hanging about his neck, and in his right foot he held a sceptre extended, and offering it to the King. . . . And across, at the foot of the Bridge, was erected the fabric of a tower, the height of the aforesaid columns, and painted; in the midst of which, under a superb tabernacle, stood a most beautiful effigy of St George, all in armour, excepting his head, which was adorned with laurel interwoven with gems, which shone between it like precious stones for their brightness. Behind him [St George] was a tapestry of cotton, having his arms resplendently embroidered in a multitude of escutcheons. Upon his right was suspended his triumphal helmet; upon his left side his shield of arms; and he had in his right hand the handle of his sword, which was girt about him. Upon the tower was raised an extended scroll, containing these words: *To God only be honour and glory;* and in front of the building this congratulatory prophecy: (Psalm xlvi) *The streams of the River made glad the City of God."*

The above conveys but a portion of the decorations which welcomed Henry V on London Bridge, the whole extent of which would surely have surprised more modern pageant-masters of our old City.

But alas, as was written in his "Elegy" by poet Thomas Gray (born, incidentally, within a few hundred yards of London Bridge):

> *The boast of heraldry, the pomp of power,*
> *And all that beauty, all that wealth e'er gave,*
> *Await alike th'inevitable hour,*
> *The paths of glory lead but to the grave.*

In a very few years Henry V was dead. He died at Vincennes near Paris, which was not quite the end expected of so venturesome a monarch. He had made many conquests in France and had been "but a step from the French throne"; but these conquests, with the exception of Calais, were due to crumble in the next reign. However, the Londoners were to know nothing of this yet, but regarded Henry V as virtually having "given France to the English". No wonder they decided to give Henry's body the splendid, though melancholy, welcome which they thought due to it. The body was laid in a chariot drawn by four great horses, and here is an account of the event quoted in Knight's *London*, 1851:

"Above the body was a figure made of boiled hides or leather representing his person, as nigh to the semblance of him as could be devised, painted curiously to the similitude of a living creature, upon whose head was set an imperial diadem of gold and precious stones; on his body a purple robe fitted with ermine, and in his right hand he held a sceptre royal, and in his left hand a ball of gold with a cross fixed thereon; and in this manner adorned was this figure laid in a bed in the said chariot, with his visage uncovered towards the heavens; and the coverture of his bed was of red silk beaten with gold.

"The chariot was surrounded by three hundred torch-bearers habited in white; by five thousand men-at-arms on horseback in black armour, holding their spears reversed. . . . After the body followed the servants of the Household all in black; then came James I of Scotland, as Chief Mourner, with the Princes and Lords of the Royal blood; and lastly, in the rear, followed Queen Catherine."

Henry V was succeeded by his infant son, Henry VI, who "ruled" under a council of regency. Henry was a weak though not a bad king, but he had not much of a chance, for his adulthood saw him engulfed in the complications of the Wars of the Roses during which, after many vicissitudes, he was imprisoned and murdered.

The reader may be wondering what all this has to do with London Bridge, but the reason for Henry VI's inclusion here is that after his coronation in France at the age of ten he was brought to London City by the usual, but not unexciting, route of London Bridge via Southwark. Presumably he had not been in England since his birth in 1421, and the Londoners were full of excitement when he appeared here as their lawful king in 1431. They were also probably tired of dull councils and duller would-be protectors, and decided to give the young king a colourful welcome. Pageants now seemed to be running to a pattern, particularly as regarded effigies. Thus Stow, that indefatigable chronicler, tells us that "when the King was come to the bridge, there was devised a mighty giant, standing with a sword drawn in his hand, having written certain speeches in metre of great rejoicing and welcoming the King to the City, on the midst of the Bridge".

The scene was well described by the monk-poet John Lydgate, a contemporary of Chaucer. He wrote various poems about the pageants on London Bridge, notably on the return of Henry V from Agincourt and the arrival of the young Henry VI after his coronation in France. John Lydgate was a monk of the Benedictine order of Bury St Edmunds, and, according to old engravings, looked the part. He wrote narrative poems, fables, allegories, and excelled in his descriptions of pageants. Much of his work was of great length, as was his poem about the young Henry VI, which runs to more than 200 lines, all of them valid poetry. Even today students of early verse and metre turn to Lydgate for study. Here is the first verse of his poem about Henry VI on London Bridge, which corresponds with the description taken from Stow. The reader will understand why more of this long poem is not set before him!

> *First, when they passyd, was ye Fabour*
> *Entring ye Brigge of this noble Towne,*
> *There was a peler reysyd like a Tour**
> *And thereon stod a sturdy champyoun,*
> *Of look and chere stern as a lyoun.*
> *His sword, up rered prowdly, 'gan manace*
> *All foreyn enemyes from the King to enehace.*

Lydgate's writings, verse and otherwise, were often attacked by other writers during his life and afterwards, though probably out of jealousy. He was even called by Ritson "a voluminous, prosaick and drivelling monk". Nevertheless – and this is what concerns us here – he wrote three long, stirring and deeply descriptive poems on three of the greatest pageants to pass over London Bridge.

In due course there was to be further pageantry on London Bridge to welcome the French bride of the same Henry VI – Margaret of Anjou, a forceful woman destined to play a great

---

* A pillar raised like a Tower

part in the history of those times. They were the times of the Wars of the Roses, and Margaret involved herself, even to the extent of organising armies and accompanying them in the field. Thus, when the battle of Tewkesbury was lost to the Yorkists, she was captured and imprisoned. Five years later she was released and returned to France. During most of her activities her husband, Henry VI, was insane – in fits and starts.

We must, however, say a few words about the pageantry which met her when she entered London as a preliminary to marrying Henry at Titchfield Abbey. Margaret had stayed at Eltham Palace in Kent on her journey from the coast, under the escort of the duke of Gloucester and a retinue. She was to be crowned at Westminster Abbey by the archbishop of Canterbury. A series of pageants welcomed her on her progress through the City, but the principal one was at the Southwark gate of London Bridge. This had "Peace and Plenty" as its theme, whilst on the bridge itself was a huge representation of Noah's Ark, bearing numerous scriptural quotations in Latin, one of them, on translation, proclaiming "There shall no more be a curse upon the earth" (Genesis, viii, 21). Not, perhaps, a very prophetic quotation in view of the Wars of the Roses soon to come, wherein much of England's nobility perished in battle.

The last royal princess to be greeted with pageantry on London Bridge was Catherine of Aragon, who came to London to marry Prince Arthur, elder son and heir of Henry VII. She became one of the saddest figures in English history. Prince Arthur died within a year of her marriage to him in St Paul's Cathedral. Arthur's brother Henry now became the heir and in due course became Henry VIII of England. Catherine, who had remained in this country, was betrothed to him, and later married him. Readers will be all too familiar with the manner in which Henry treated her, contriving ingeniously to have her marriage set aside in favour of Anne Boleyn. Catherine was allowed to stay in England, and, according to one account of her, she was deprived of friends and died in solitude at Kimbolton in Huntingdonshire, having spent her days in prayer and needlework. She had outlived her arch-enemy, Cardinal Wolsey, by some six years, so she may have derived some satisfaction from the stories of his humiliation which reached her.

The pageantry which greeted her on London Bridge no doubt followed the general pattern of such occasions, though on a smaller scale than that accorded to Margaret of Anjou, for she came as a princess and not a queen. It is, however, worth quoting old Stow on the matter: "About two of the clock at afternoon, the said Princess, accompanied with many lords and ladies, in most sumptuous manner apparelled, came riding from Lambeth into Southwark, and so to London Bridge, where was ordained a costly pageant of St Katherine and St Ursula, with many virgins." Actually, this was the first of at least six pageants which greeted her in her procession through the City. Alas, poor Catherine!

The next and the last pageant to be mentioned here took place a good two hundred years after the one mentioned above, but that does not mean that there were none in the intervening period. Far from it, but we have confined ourselves here to pageants of state or historical importance, such as the following, which was a pageant to welcome King Charles II on his return from exile at the Restoration. Those drab Puritan years had been a little too much for the London citizens, by nature cheerful both then and now. They welcomed their lively king "with hearts and hands and voices".

Here is an account of the occasion as given in the *Chronicles of London Bridge*:

"About three in the afternoon the King arrived in Southwark, and thence proceeded over the Bridge into the City, attended by all the glory of London, and the military forces of the kingdom. . . . The procession, which was chiefly an equestrian one, was begun by soldiers, and 300 Citizens in cloth of silver doublets; who were followed by 1200 more all in velvet, with footmen and liveries in purple. Then came other parties habited in buff coats with sleeves of silver tissue and green silk scarfs. . . . Eighty of the Sheriffs' followers attended in red cloaks lined with silver, holding half-pikes; and 600 of the City Companies in black velvet cloaks and gold chains. . . . Then came the City Marshall with eight footmen in French green trimmed with crimson and white; whilst the City Waits and Officers, the Sheriffs, the Aldermen, and their attendants blazed in red, and cloths of gold and silver, in the next rank. Heralds and Maces,

13. The coffer dam superstructure, prepared for spectators, and decorated with flags in honour of the laying of the foundation stone of Rennie's London Bridge.

14. Interior of the coffer dam. The foundation stone is suspended above a cavity for coins, etc. (bottom right).

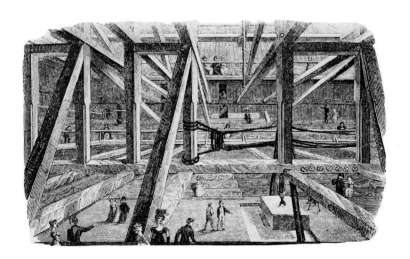

15 and 16. Rennie's London Bridge, begun in 1824.
(Above) Workmen proceed with their perilous tasks
which cost some forty lives. (Below) The lord mayor's
procession passing under the unfinished arches on
9 November 1827.

17 and 18. Two London Bridges, the new and the old,
face to face. The view above is from the City, the
other from Southwark.

19. William IV at the forefront of the procession at the opening of the new London Bridge, 1 August 1831.

20. The scene below the bridge at the opening ceremony. The vast marquee on the bridge itself was to accommodate the guests at the banquet (1831).

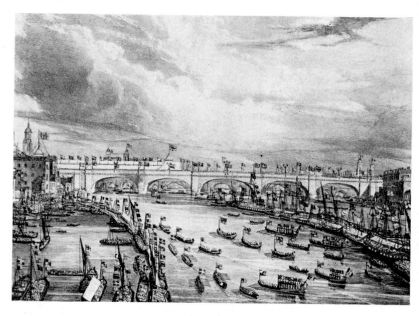

21. The Thames at its gayest. Rivercraft of all types, decorated with flags, congregate to celebrate the opening (1831).

22. Entrance to the metropolis from the new London Bridge soon after its completion. Fishmongers' Hall is on the left.

23. Attempt to blow up London Bridge by the "Dyna-
miters" in December 1884; from a contemporary
periodical.

24. Old Swan Wharf, Bridge Master's Office and Fishmongers' Hall and its wharf.

25. The Worshipful Livery Company of Vintners owns these swans which gather on the Thames foreshore.

in their splendid habits, preceded by Sir Thomas Allen, the Lord Mayor; who, to gratify the City, was permitted to carry the sword of London immediately before the King, which had not been done in any former public entry, excepting when Charles I returned from Scotland in 1641, and even then the Sword of State had the precedence."

Fig. 6. James I in a Thames procession. The water-stairs in the background were for the use of the occupants of the houses who used water traffic.

6

FIRE—FLOOD—FROST

Until we remember the many centuries during which London Bridge – timber or stone – spanned the Thames, we might think it had more than its share of vicissitude. Such is the effect of foreshortening history. Actually, some of the frowns of fortune mentioned here had intervals of many scores of years between them. Nevertheless, even the interims seem to have provided a succession of minor, though costly troubles. This applied especially to the later years of Old London Bridge, when the hands of the authorities were rarely out of their pockets. Some of these "running expenses" are mentioned in our book, but the present chapter concerns the more spectacular happenings which must have caused much lively talk at the time, and kept the upkeep of the bridge at a high level.

Of course, many of the disasters which befell the earlier timber bridges were visited upon them by the Danes; the others were brought about by fire and flood. We know but little of them, for record-keeping in those illiterate days was, to say the least, perfunctory. Moreover, a damaged timber bridge was easily restored. We are told, however, that in 1091 a great gale struck the whole City and destroyed some six hundred houses and a number of churches. Among the latter was St Mary-le-Bow in Cheapside, parts of which remain to this day, beneath the present structure. A short account in the *Chronicles of London Bridge* (1839) tells an odd story: "The roof was carried to a considerable distance, and fell with such force, that several of the rafters being about twenty-eight feet long, pierced upwards of twenty feet into the ground, and remained in the same position as when they stood in the Chapel."

Another account (originally in the *Chronicles* of Florence of Worcester, a very ancient book) tells us that during the same storm the water in the Thames rushed along with such rapidity, and increased so violently, that London Bridge was entirely swept away; while the lands on each side were flooded for a considerable distance. The credit for rebuilding the bridge is generally ascribed to William Rufus, who reigned from 1087 to 1100. Much of the money for this restoration may well have come from levies on lands in the counties of Surrey and Middlesex. Stow quotes a charter from Henry I (who succeeded Rufus in 1100). This charter exempts a certain manor belonging to the monks of Battle Abbey from "shires and hundreds and all other customs of earthly servitude, and namely, from the work of London Bridge. . . ." Apparantly the monks and their manor had done their bit by the time Rufus was killed by an arrow in the New Forest.

But this new bridge was not to last long, as bridges go, for no sooner had Henry I breathed his last than fire laid hold of it and destroyed it. This was in the first year of the reign of King Stephen. It was no local fire, but engulfed a good part of the City. According to Stow in his Survey, "A fire began in the house of one Ailwarde, near unto London Stone, which consumed east to Aldgate, and west to St Erkenwald's tome in Powle's [St Paul's] church; the bridge of timber over the river of Thames was also burnt, but afterwards again repaired." No doubt it was, for the contemporary historian, FitzStephen, writing a little later, speaks of when "pastimes were showed on the river Thames, and men stood in great number on the Bridge, wharfs and houses to behold". It would appear that the repairs to the bridge were only temporary, for later Peter de Colechurch* rebuilt it entirely, presumably acting as architect. This bridge served its purpose for some thirteen years, when the priest-architect began his celebrated stone bridge which lasted for about six centuries and which, in times nearer our own, came to be called Old London Bridge.

This bridge took thirty-three years to complete, but the demon Fire had its eye on it, and not long after its completion, by which time there were numerous buildings upon it, a conflagration broke out in the church of St Mary Overie near the foot of the bridge. This fire spread to the bridge and destroyed three arches out of the twenty, and also the chapel of

* See Chapter 3

St Thomas à Becket. But this was not the extent of the catastrophe. "Within four years," says Stow, "after the finishing of the Bridge, to wit, in the year 1212, on the 10th of July at night, the borough of Southwark, upon the south side of the River Thames, as also the church of Our Lady of Canons [i.e. St Mary Overies] there, being on fire, and an exceeding great multitude of people passing the Bridge, either to extinguish or quench it, or else to gaze at and behold it, suddenly the north part, by blowing of the south wind was also set on fire, and the people which were even now passing the Bridge, perceiving the same, would have returned, but were stopped by the fire; and it came to pass that as they stayed or protracted time, the other end of the Bridge, namely the south end, was fired, so that the people thronging themselves between the two fires, did nothing else but to expect present death; then came there to aid them many ships and vessels, into which the multitude so unadvisedly rushed, that the ships being drowned, they all perished. It is said that, through the fire and shipwreck, there were destroyed about *three thousand persons*, whose bodies were found in part, or half burnt, besides those that were wholly burnt to ashes, and could not be found."

The bridge remained in a ruinous condition for many years, though available for restricted traffic. Harben, in his *Dictionary of London*, remarks that "the Bridge seems always to have been a costly structure to maintain, partly on account of the storms and fires that desolated it from time to time, and partly on account of the weight of the buildings erected upon it. From early times rents and lands were appropriated for its repair and upkeep, while the bequests made by the citizens of London for this purpose were surprisingly numerous and munificent."

Another enemy of the bridge was frost, which was ever liable to strike terror into those living on the bridge. Thus Stow tells us in his Survey that "about the year 1282, through a great frost and deep snow, five arches of London Bridge were borne down and carried away". Stow says no more about this frost; nor do other histories. With five arches completely disappeared there was, presumably, little more to be said! The main story here, as the newspapers of today would say, lay in the steps taken to reconstruct the bridge which was already in a parlous state, as recounted elsewhere.

There were, of course, high doings on the Thames during the great frosts. It was a regular practice for small printers to set up their presses on the ice and charge folk for their names printed "on the Thames". Among those to patronise one printer, G. Croom, were King Charles II, Queen Katherine and the duke of York. Master Croom's printed sheet bearing their names bears the imprint: "London; Printed by G. Croom, on the ICE, on the River of Thames, January 31, 1684." This, or something like it, was a common imprint of printers who set up their very temporary presses on the frozen Thames.

Fires, frosts and floods plagued London Bridge almost in rotation. There was one fire, not confined to the bridge but also to a good portion of the City, which does not receive as much attention as it should in history, perhaps because it occurred only thirty years or so before the Great Fire of London of 1666 which, of course, became the undying news story of London. This was the fire of 1633, which broke out near St Magnus Church, in the house of one Brigges, a needle-maker, on account, it was said, of a maidservant placing some hot coals under a wooden staircase. Connoisseurs of coincidences will be struck by the similarity between this fire and the Great Fire of London which began in Pudding Lane, close to the church of St Magnus, and was caused by hot ashes setting alight the tinder-dry flooring of a baker's house at that spot.

The fire of 1633 was one of the most memorable ever to assail Old London Bridge. The best account of it which I have found is based on the diary of one Nehemiah Wallington, who worked as a turner (some say needle-maker) in Little Eastcheap and actually witnessed the fire. He was a super-dedicated Puritan, and saw the benign hand of God in even the most terrible disasters. There have been various "translations" of the quaint English in which he wrote his accounts and opinions. There latter appeared in a large volume under the title of *Record of the Mercies of God, or a Thoughtful Remembrance*. I give here a modified version of an extract from the *Chronicles of London Bridge*:

"1633. It is the bounden dutie of ye all that have beene the beholders of the wonderful workes of the Lord our God, his mercies and judgments shewed heretofore; and now of late of a fearefull fire, we should not forgett itt ourselves, and we should declare it to all others, even to ye generations to come. On the sixth day of February began, by God's just hand, a fearfull fire in the house of Mr John Brigges near tenn of the clock att night, it burnt down his house and the next one to itt, with all the goods which were in them; and, as I heare, that Brigges, his wife and child, escaped with their lives very hardly, having nothing on their bodies but their shirt and smoke; and the fire burnt so fearcely, that it could not be quenched till it had burnt downe all the houses on both sides of the way [i.e. London Bridge], from S. Magnus Church to the first open place. And although there was water enough very neere, yet they could not safely come at it, but all the conduits neere were opened, and the pipes that carried water through the streets were cut open, and the watter swept down with broomes with helpe enough; but it was the will of God that it should not prevaile. And the hand of God was the more seen in this, in as much as no meanes would prosper [i.e. that nothing could be done?]."

Then comes an interesting reference to fire engines:

"For the 3 engines, which are such excellent things, that nothing that was ever devised could do so much good, yet none of these did prosper, for they were all broken, and the tide was verie low that they could get no watter; and the pipes that were cutt yeilded but littel watter. Some ladders were broke to the hurt of many, for some had their legges broke, some had their arms and some their ribbes broke, and many lost their lives. This fire burnt fiercely all night and part of next day till all was burned and pulled downe to the grounde. Yet the timber and wood and coales in the sellars could not be quenched all that week, for I was there then my selfe, and had a live coal in my hand and burnt my finger with it. Notwithstanding, there were as many night and day as could labour one by another to carry away timber, and brickes and tiles and rubbish cast down into the liter [lighyers?]. So that on Wensday the Bridge was cleared that passengers might goe over."

Apparently this temporary clearing-up took but a few days, which was a remarkably energetic piece of work, especially when it is remembered that no fewer than forty-six houses were demolished, as is stated in another account. Old Nehemiah (and it is difficult to imagine a young Nehemiah!) kept up the Scriptural reputation of his forebear to the end of his account, which concludes:

"It did make me think of that fire which the Lord threatened against Jerusalem, for the breach of his Sabbath day. He said thus: 'But if ye will not heare me to sanctify the Sabbath day, and to bear no burden, nor to go through the gates of Jerusalem on ye Sabbath day, then will I kindle a fire in the gates, and it shall devoure the palaces of Jerusalem, and it shall not be quenched.' "*

He does, however, add a less forbidding note when he says:

"I did heere that on the other side of the Bridge, the Bruers brought an abundance of watters on their draies, which did, with the blessing of God, much good; and this mircie of God I much thought on that there was littel wind, for had the wind been as high as it was the weekes before, I think it would have indangered the most part of the Citie, for in Thames Street there is much pitch, tarre and oile in their houses. Therefore, as God remembers mercy in justice, let us remember thankfulness in sorrow . . . for it is of the Lord's mercy that we are not consumed."

Severe and prolonged frosts on the Thames in those days ran somewhat to a pattern, and often meant no more than that hordes of people crowded the bridge to look down on the merrymaking on the ice below, which included football, dancing, bonfires, bear-baiting, ox-roasting and the like. One of the notable exceptions was the great frost of the comparatively recent year of 1785. It lasted for 115 days, during which the whole river was disorganised. The Thames watermen provided an amusing diversion to this serious event. They were, of course, deprived of their usual occupation as ferrymen, so as compensation they broke the shore-side ice at various places and erected small bridges over which people might pass to the main ice for a toll of a halfpenny each.

This, however, was but one of the lighter facets. A more

* The quotation is from Jeremiah, xvii, 27

serious side was shown in the freezing out of action of the great water-works at the end of the bridge, which pumped water to the citizens of the City and, in another case, of Southwark. (These water-works and their origin are described fully in our Miscellany.) It became the work of voluntary citizens and paid workers several times a day to heat large quantities of water and pour it from the bridge on to the water-works. This was no simple task, for the water had to be heated over coal fires. Still, the energies of the workers were not fruitless, and it was contrived to keep the wheels turning and the pumps working.

Eventually the thaw came, but it was far from an unmixed blessing, for it brought calamities far in excess of those of a frozen, static river. The only comforting thought was that a thaw is usually of short duration, whereas, with a frost – well, you never can tell! The usual precursor of a thaw is, as any country skater will tell us, an ominous cracking of the ice. In our case not every reveller on the ice would believe that the end of the frost was at hand, but, when this came to be realised at eight o'clock one night, there was an outburst of stampedes, and confusion set in. The ordinary revellers quickly made their way to the banks of the river on either side; but those who had booths and puppet shows and even owners of bulls and bears for baiting were loth to leave their property to the mercy of the creaking and growling ice. It would need another Nehemiah Wallington to interpret the ways of Providence during those tense, panic-stricken hours. Suffice it to say that everyone reached the shores safely, though quite a few had to leave their goods behind them.

Thaws, moreover, always provided their perils to the bridge's structure, for they brought enormous floating pieces of ice, sometimes $1\frac{1}{2}$ feet thick and of great weight. On one occasion the force of the ice-floes was so great that a French merchant-man was flung against the sterlings, losing its bowsprit and part of the superstructure, so that it had to be secured by ropes until conditions rendered its salvage possible. Other ships suffered similar disasters, some even losing their mainmasts against the arches. The bridge itself, of course, suffered on these occasions, some of the piers being concussed into insecurity. One of the remedies applied was the pouring of hundreds of tons of Kentish ragstone into the water around the piles. It was not a satisfactory process as it impeded navigation under the arches, but it had its immediate uses.

Reverting to fires, the next one we shall mention will be the Great Fire of London in 1666, but a year before that London had to endure the Great Plague, one of the greatest calamities to strike any city in this country or any other. For the horrific details of this pestilence we must refer the reader to *A Journal of the Plague Year*, attributed to Daniel Defoe, although the most accepted copy is stated to have been written "by a Citizen who continued all the while in London" and "Never been Made Public before". There had been two previous plagues in that same century, in 1603 and 1625, in which respectively, in London alone, 33,000 and 41,000 people perished. In the Great Plague, however, the fatalities in London were 68,000. There is in the old records very scant reference to the effects of the Plague on the inhabitants of London Bridge, and such as there are are conflicting. In one of the latter it is claimed that "the inhabitants of the Bridge were free from its ravages; which is attributed to the ceaseless rushing of the river below it". This theory has been so often discounted that we may just as well discount it here. Defoe's book seems to come nearest in linking the Plague with the bridge, though not actually mentioning the latter. Defoe (assuming that he was the author), in speaking of the numerous fires which were lit about the City to purify it, says "I do not remember whether there was any one at the City Gates, but one at the Bridge foot there was, just by St Magnus church". (I should mention that Defoe was but an infant at the time of the Plague, and the words quoted above could only have been those which he put into the mouth of the Citizen on whom he pinned his book many years afterwards.)

The City had only a short respite before it was engulfed by the Great Fire of London which, as mentioned above, started in Pudding Lane, close by St Magnus Church near the foot of the bridge. There are numerous accounts of the conflagration, including those by Samuel Pepys and Sir John Evelyn, those two diarists beyond compare. Evelyn says little about the effect of the Fire on the actual bridge, though he remarks that had the Fire ignited the gunpowder store in the Tower of London nearby it might well have blown up London Bridge. Pepys speaks of seeing houses burning at the end of the bridge, but without saying that they were on the bridge itself. It is clear from other reports, however, that quite a number of buildings on the north (or City) end of the bridge were burned down.

The Great Fire of London just mentioned occurred in 1666, after which London Bridge enjoyed a respite from the ravages of its old enemy, Fire, for nearly a century – until 1758, the year which marked the restoration of the bridge and the removal of the buildings which stood upon it. A temporary bridge of timber had been erected alongside to ensure the continuance of traffic during the operation, and on an April night of the above year it was destroyed by a fire which was generally attributed to arson. This fire, and the rumours which derived from it, is described fully in Chapter 9.

7

REBELS AT THE GATE

As we have seen elsewhere, Southwark was the all-in-one arrival and departure "platform" for the important traffic – state and otherwise – to and from France via the Dover Road, and for the ever-increasing comings and goings of the "commercial vehicles" of Kent, Surrey and Sussex. It also provided temporary sojourn for a mixed assortment of dubious folk intent on exploiting the City. Among these, in mass numbers, were the rebels renowned in history – political and social – who over a century or two crossed, or tried to cross, London Bridge and thus attain the capital. They included Jack Cade, Lord Falconbridge (the Bastard of Falconbridge), Sir Thomas Wyatt and Wat Tyler. It is not difficult to imagine the alarm of the citizens, living peacefully in their medieval London, on learning that there was a well-armed mob battering at their gate, the gate being at the Southwark end of London Bridge.*

The most notable of the rebels was Jack Cade, and Cade's Rebellion remains one of the highlights of London's history, and well it might, for it entailed the fiercest of battles that the bridge ever knew. Jack Cade and Wat Tyler are often bracketed together, yet their rebellions were basically different, that of the former being political and the other social.

Tyler's insurrection took place a year or two after the introduction of the Poll Tax into England and on account of it. There was nothing new about the Poll Tax. Even the Greeks had it. It was a tax of so much a head on every man and woman in the country, excepting beggars. In Tyler's time the tax was

---

* It will be noticed that I am not including among the rebels the Danes and others who persistently harried the timber bridges of earlier days. Those mentioned in this chapter applied their attentions to the stone bridge of Peter de Colechurch. The Danes were foes, not rebels.

fourpence per head, and it must be remembered that fourpence
in those days was no mean sum for working people to pay;
hence the rural dissatisfaction which preceded Tyler's move in
1381, which, however, had its more intimate side. Tyler, who
was said to have been a tiler of Dartford, was a married man
with a wife and family which included a daughter, and a pretty
one at that. On the occasion of the tax-man calling to collect
the Poll Tax trouble blew up when the tax-man tried to take
advantage of the girl, whereupon Wat Tyler killed him on the
spot. All the people were on Wat's side and, the discontent
being what it was, a body of men, led by Tyler and Jack Straw,
started to march to London from Kent. (This was the Jack
Straw who, with a party of Tyler's rebels, burnt down a small
mansion, the ruins of which became known as Jack Straw's
Castle; hence the name of the famous inn near Hampstead.)

In due course Tyler and his followers, who were greatly
augmented on the way, arrived in Southwark and encamped
there prior to making a forced entry over London Bridge. They
appear to have had a high old time in Southwark, pillaging
right and left. In particular they damaged and otherwise maltreated the Southwark "stews", or brothels, for which Southwark was then notorious. There was a doubtful touch of humour
about this, for the stews belonged to no other than London's
lord mayor, Sir William Walworth, who rented them to "the
fraus of Flanders", and who was eventually to run his dagger
through Wat Tyler, perhaps not without relish in view of what
had happened at Southwark!

Meanwhile the "commons" of Surrey had marched up and
joined Tyler, so that he was now in command of a considerable
number of followers. There are various accounts of how Tyler
crossed London Bridge, a matter made difficult by the same
William Walworth who had raised the drawbridge and stretched
a strong iron chain across the approach to it. But this did not
deter the rebels, who "cried to the wardens of the Bridge to let
it down and give them entry, whereby they might pass, or else
they would destroy them all, whereby they were constrained by
fear to let it down and give them entry – at which time the
religious present were earnest in procession and prayer for
peace". (This probably refers to the priests in the chapel of
St Thomas à Becket on the bridge. No doubt they interspersed

their prayers for peace with a few silent ones for their own safety!)

Certainly Tyler and his men crossed the bridge to the City side and made their way to Mile End, in what we now call the East End, and encamped there on the Green. Meanwhile the boy king, Richard II, and his ministers scowled within the Tower, less than a mile away. It was decided to send the young king to parley, and he was escorted on horseback to meet the rebels, whom he greatly impressed by his bravery. Acting on instructions, Richard promised Tyler and his men to repeal the Poll Tax and put an end to serfdom – a promise his wily advisers never intended to perform. Many of the peasants returned to their homes. Tyler, however, led the others into London. Many of them ran riot, looting what they wished and killing whom they had a mind to – including the archbishop of Canterbury.

A further meeting was called at West Smithfield, with young Richard again to the fore. Tyler by this time was so swollen-headed that he chose to make an insulting remark to the king. This was too much for Walworth, the lord mayor, who ran his dagger into the impudent rebel. Wat Tyler was carried, dead or dying, into St Bartholomew's hospital, founded by the monk Rahere a couple of centuries even before that. After this episode the Peasants' Revolt collapsed.

There are some grisly recollections attached to Mile End Green, for it was a much-fancied spot for the erection of gibbets. Various suspected traitors, some of them courtiers, were executed there, and their bodies exhibited on gibbets; not that all the gibbets bore the aristocratic stamp, as did the poles on London Bridge. Far from it, for, in corners of the great common, thieves, cut-purses, highwaymen and such were hanged and their bodies left to rot in chains. River pirates, of course, were dealt with at Execution Dock, almost in sight of London Bridge, there to be tied to posts on the foreshore at *low* tide and left till two *high* tides had submerged them.

Sir William Walworth was a member of the Fishmongers' Company, and his dagger rests in their livery hall* at the foot of London Bridge, displayed on an embroidered Tudor pall. In

*Fishmongers' Hall is dealt with in the Miscellany, as is also the church of St Magnus the Martyr almost adjoining the bridge

the livery hall, too, is a chair made from one of the piles of old London Bridge (plate 26). In speaking of Sir William Walworth's dagger in the Fishmongers' Hall I mention the oft-discussed dagger on the City of London flag which always flutters chirpily from the radiator of the lord mayor's car when he goes about his duties in the City. The flag is that of St George, plain white and a large red cross from edges to edges, similar to the device of the Crusaders, but with a dagger gleaming red in the first quarter. This weapon is generally associated with Sir William Walworth, but, as I have written later on, there is much more than a doubt about it.

Jack Cade and his insurgent followers were the most violent ever to attack London Bridge from Southwark. There is some obscurity about Cade's origin. Some accounts say that he was a scallywag who left Ireland to escape the consequences of murdering a pregnant woman, but the more credible one is that he was of Kentish stock and a small landowner, like so many who supported him. This seems verified by the fact that, presumably after his death, his possessions came within the terms of the Act of Attainder by which a man found guilty of treason or felony of a capital kind had his lands forfeited. (Attainder was abolished in 1870, having lasted from the reign of Edward II.) Cade, incidentally, took to himself the name of Mortimer and claimed some connection with royalty.

I have said that Cade's insurrection was political as compared with that of Wat Tyler. There had been considerable discontent in England before Cade's activities. This was partly due to the whittling away of Henry V's conquests in France by those acting for his successor, Henry VI, who, for much of his reign, was beset by fits of madness. Our armies in France were for long under the command of the duke of Suffolk (the fourth of his line) who at one point effected a truce with France and managed to marry Henry VI to Margaret of Anjou who, despite her fierce allegiance to her husband, was highly unpopular with the English people. Soon the duke of York, head of a branch of the royal line, became active in the scene and schemed to take the crown from Henry. Such were the various affairs which made England a land of discontent, a land ready for Cade's Rebellion, or so it seemed.

Once having decided on insurrection it did not take Jack

Cade (we will forget the Mortimer) long to gather a strong band of malcontents and march towards London, gathering hundreds more at each point of his march. He was held up at Sevenoaks by a detachment of the king's troops under Sir Humphrey Stafford, but by an adroit ambush he defeated them into helplessness, killing their leader in the process. After a brief encampment at Blackheath he made his way to Southwark and encamped there at the very gate of the City, soon to be joined by the rebels of Essex who had mustered at Mile End Green, the scene of Wat Tyler's first meeting with King Richard II. The storm clouds were now gathering fast.

Stow in his Survey says, speaking of Southwark, ". . . from thence towards London Bridge, on the same side, be many fair inns for receipt of travellers, by these signs, the Spurre, Christopher, Bull, Queen's Head, Tabard, George, Hart, etc.". Stow enlarges on the Tabard as the headquarters of the Canterbury Pilgrims, but says nothing about the Hart, though this was the inn wherein Jack Cade took up his abode on the fateful night of his arrival in Southwark.

Stow tells us that Cade was informed that "he might not be suffered to enter the Citie". But Cade had not marched his rebel rout from Kent to obey prohibitions of that kind. Moreover, this being a political rebellion, Cade was not without friends – even accomplices – in the City. Indeed it was said that many of the Train[ed] Bands, or citizen soldiers, were in his favour.

Readers may recall the first verse of Cowper's famous poem about John Gilpin, the adventurous haberdasher:

> *John Gilpin was a citizen of credit and renown;*
> *A Train Band captain eke was he,*
> *Of famous London Town.*

The Train Bands, as such, were constituted in the reign of James I, but as they ranged themselves with the Parliamentarians in the Civil War, they found themselves disbanded by Charles II when he returned to his late father's kingdom at the Restoration. Whether the Train Bands supported Cade or not we cannot be sure, but it seems certain that some "fifth column" was at work, for when he essayed to cross the bridge he found the gates open to him. As he crossed the drawbridge, followed by his "forces", he cut the supporting ropes of the bridge with his own sword. Thus was the situation to which Shakespeare chose to refer in *Henry VI*:

> *Jack Cade hath gotten London Bridge; the citizens*
> *Fly and forsake their houses.*

Certainly Cade crossed the bridge, burning a number of houses on his way and causing the death of many inhabitants. But he was imprudent enough, or rapacious enough, to commit several robberies when he entered the City. This aroused the ire of the citizens and civic authorities, so that a little further in this story we find Jack Cade back again at the Southwark end of the bridge. Then began the battle proper, for the City captains, the mayor, aldermen and commonality of London mounted guard upon the bridge. We will draw upon Hall, the historian from Shropshire, for what happened next, though slightly modernising his picturesque wording:

"The rebelles, which never soundly slept, for fear of sudden chances, hearing the bridge to be kept and manned, ran with greate haste to open the passage, where between both parties was a ferce and cruell encounter. Matthew Gough, more expert in martial feates than the other Chieftains of the Citie, perceiving the Kentishmen better to stand tackling than he had imagined, advised his company to proceed no farther toward Southwarke, till the day appeared (so that Citizens and their friends might withdraw). But this counseil came to little effect, for the multitude of rebelles drave the Citizens from the Bridge foote, to the draw-bridge, and began to set fire to divers houses.

"Alas, what sorrow it was to beholde that miserable chaunce; for some desiring to eschew the fyre leapt on his enemies weapon, and so died; fearful women, with chyldren in their arms, amazed and appalled lept into the river; others, doubting how they might save themselves between fyre, water and sword, were in their houses suffocate and smoldered, yet the Captaines [City] nothing regarding these chaunces, fought on this draw-bridge all the nyghte valiantly, but in conclusion the rebelles got the drawbridge and drowned many, and slew John Sutton, Alderman, and Heysande, a hardy Citizen, with many other besyde Matthew Gough, a man of great witte, much experience in feates of chivalry, the which in continuall warres had

valiantly served the King and his father in the partes beyond
the seas. But it is often the same, that he which many times both
vanquished his enemies in strange countryes and returned
again as a conqueror, hath of his own nation afterward been
shamefully murdered and brought to confusion. [An observation which throws some light on Hall's human outlook.]

"This hard and sore conflict endured on the Bridge til ix. of
the clocke in the mornynge in doubtful chaunce and Fortune's
balaunce. For some time the Londoners were set back to
St Magnus Corner [i.e. the city end of the bridge], and suddenly
again the rebelles were repulsed and driven back to the
Southern end of the Bridge, so that both parties being faynte,
weary and fatygate, agreed to desist from fight, and to leave
battle till the next day, upon condition that neyther Londoners
should passe into Southwarke, nor the Kentish men into
London."

During the truce which followed this most valiant defence of
London Bridge, observes the *Chronicles* of the same, and which
nearly effaced the deep stain of the Citizens opening their gates
to a rebel, a general pardon was procured for Cade and his
followers by John Stafford, archbishop of Canterbury, Lord
High Chancellor. Upon which some accepted the king's grace
and began by degrees to withdraw from Southwark with their
spoils. Cade refused to acknowledge defeat (some say with
reason) and took to the country where, with some followers, he
fell fighting at Heathfield in Sussex. There was no mercy now,
and it is hardly necessary to say that his head ultimately
appeared on a pole on London Bridge. The same happened to
a score or so of his followers who were taken with him.

Less than a score of years after Cade's attack on the City
came another insurgent, responsible, like Cade, for bloodshed
on the bridge. Strangely, the episode seems largely unknown to
people nowadays, people to whom Wat Tyler and Jack Cade
are familiar figures of the mind; yet it was far from being un-
important. The leader of the attempt on London was one,
Neville, known as the Bastard of Falconbridge (or Faulcon-
bridge), so named because he was the natural son of Lord
Falconbridge, one of the Nevilles of the powerful Warwick
family, headed by Warwick "the Kingmaker".

At the time of which we write the Wars of the Roses were rife with all their complications of royal strategies and intrigues which we will not attempt to probe here. Falconbridge, as Neville came to be called, was an adherent of the deranged Henry VI who was periodically in confinement or captivity. Falconbridge is recorded as a worthless fellow, but he had enough about him to raise a number of ships and 3,000 followers in order to liberate Henry VI, or so he proclaimed, though plunder of the capital may not have been far from his mind, nor from those of his supporters.

He had his ships brought up the Thames to near the bridge, whilst he marched his "army" into Southwark, of which he took possession, or nearly so. He also ordered a large force to cross the river in boats and to take hold of Aldgate and Bishopsgate on the northern side of the Thames. In short, he was trying to stage a large-scale siege of the City.

In his attack on London Bridge itself he came up against Alderman Ralph Joceline, later lord mayor, who with his City forces defended the bridge to some purpose. All the attacks of "The Bastard" were repulsed with many losses, so that eventually the attackers withdrew and made off down the southern bank of the river, pursued by the alderman's force who captured or killed many of them. It must not go unmentioned, however, that in their various assaults on the bridge they managed to fire "a goodly number of houses" on the structure. Falconbridge's ships were moored off Rotherhithe which, it is interesting to know, was then called Redriff, a name which still lingers among the older riverside dwellers. Falconbridge and a number of his men managed to reach the ships and, presumably under cover of night, stole down the estuary and away. Some accounts say that the ships bombarded the City end of the bridge and got as good as they gave from the City ordnance, but this story should be received with caution.

For our next and last "rebel at the gate" we go to the short reign of Mary Tudor, a reign which lasted but five merciless years yet was long enough to earn for her the name "Bloody Mary" on account of her persecution of the English Protestants. But it was her marriage to Philip II of Spain which brought real anger to her people. This gentleman was anathema to the English, who even saw the threat of a Spanish Inquisition being set up in this country when he became established. There was also distaste for anything resembling vassaldom to Spain. The "rebel" concerned was Sir Thomas Wyatt, a man of courtesy as will be seen.

Sir Thomas Wyatt was the son of an English courtier, diplomat and poet, who was born at Allington Castle in Kent. He served with the army abroad and then, it is said, was ambassador in Spain. When Queen Mary was planning to marry Philip II he was the guiding spirit of the English opposition to the match and later became the instigator of a widespread conspiracy against the queen. He raised an army and marched with 4,000 men to Southwark from Kent and adjoining counties. Actually the rising was to be general, and risings were planned in various counties about the country, but Wyatt was the first to move, though an abortive effort had been made and quelled in Warwickshire. His force in Southwark was reinforced by numbers of London sympathisers including even some of the City's Train Bands. He was also equipped with ordnance.

On his appearance in Southwark, London, under the leadership of the lord mayor, Sir Thomas White, braced itself and prepared to resist. I have chosen an extract from the *Chronicles of London Bridge* (1827) for an account of the happenings:

"The Draw-Bridge at London Bridge was then cut down and thrown into the river; the Bridge gates were shut; ramparts and fortifications were raised around them; ordnance was planted to defend them; and the Mayor and Sheriffs, well armed for the conflict, commanded all persons to shut their shops and windows, and to stand ready harnessed at their doors for any event which might occur. As Wyat found there was no opposition made to him in Southwark, some of his soldiers completely sacked the Bishop of Winchester's Palace, and destroyed his extensive library; whilst at the Bridge foot he laid two pieces of ordnance and dug an extensive trench between the Bridge and his forces.

"In order to gain an entrance to the Bridge, Sir Thomas brake down the wall of a house adjoining the gate, and then coming down into the Porter's lodge, about eleven at night, he found the Porter sleeping, but his wife, with several others, watching over a coal fire. On beholding Wyat, they suddenly started, when he commanded them to be silent; and, as they loved their lives, and they would have no hurt; and, they timidly yielding to him, he and some others went upon the Bridge to reconnoitre. On the other side of the Draw-Bridge he saw the Lord Admiral, the Lord Mayor, Sir Andrew Judd, and one or two more, in consultation for defence of the Bridge, as we may suppose by fire or torchlight; and, after some time, carefully observing their deliberations, he returned to his party unseen and uninjured."

Just what Sir Thomas overheard in his courageous eavesdropping we cannot say, but it was evidently to the effect that there was awaiting him on the bridge a stronger opposition than he had anticipated, and that there were guns mounted on the Tower of London capable of firing on his "troops" should they attempt the bridge. He returned to his followers to discuss matters and, after other alternatives had been considered, it was eventually decided to march up to Kingston, there to cross the river by some means and to attack London from the west. This he proceeded to do and gained the other side. What happened to him after that scarcely comes into our story of London Bridge. Suffice it to say that he was ultimately defeated and captured, with the result that he was executed and his quarters exhibited in four parts of London. One might have expected his head to find a place among the grim collection on London Bridge, but it was fixed on a gibbet near Hyde Park from where it was stolen, probably by the supporters of the cause for which he died. I have mentioned that Wyatt was a man of courtesy, as might have been expected considering his parentage. Here, then, is a story of his gentility almost under the nose of his enemies, as culled from an old record. As we have seen, the City's ordnance was mounted on, among other places, the Tower of London, with the Southwark end of the bridge well in range. The nearby dwellers were in terror and, just before he withdrew, approached Sir Thomas in these terms: " 'Sir, we are all likely to be undone, and destroyed for your sake, our houses shall by and bye bee throwne downe upon our heads, to the utter spoil of this Borough, with the shot of the Tower, already bent and charged against us; for the love of God take pity on us.' At which wordes hee being partly abashed, stayed a while, and then sayd: 'I pray you my friends bee content for a while, and I will soone ease you of this mischief, for God forbid that you, or the least of you, should be killed, or hurt, in my behalfe.' And so, in most speedie manner, he marched away."

8

LONDON BRIDGE'S SOUTHWARK

It would not have been a misnomer to have called our bridge the Bridge of Southwark, so intimately has its history been bound up with The Borough as it has been called for two centuries or more. Certainly London Bridge was born of Southwark as is clear from Chapter 2. The first serious timber bridge was built out of the proceeds of John Audery's Southwark ferry, as was the long-lasting stone bridge started by the priest-architect, Peter de Colechurch, chaplain of a church of that name in the City, but a Southwark man by long habit.

Southwark marked the comings and goings of London

Fig. 7. Approach to London Bridge on the Southwark side.

cavalcades, military and political, in their journeys along the Dover Road which led to the coast and France. It was at the Southwark end of the bridge that Wat Tyler, Jack Cade, Sir Thomas Wyatt and other insurrectionists encamped before making their attacks on London, and it was to the Southwark Tower of the bridge that the traitors' heads were diverted from the decaying tower in the middle of the bridge in 1577. Southwark was the centre of London's intellectual drama and poetry to which throngs crossed the Thames, there to see Shakespeare, who lived there, act in his own plays.

Romance finds no place in the sombre Southwark of today, now that industry has entered its soul, but it was not always so. A glance back will show us a picturesque congestion of noble houses with overhanging gables, ripe hostelries, notorious "stews", grim prisons, teeming theatres, religious houses, pleasure gardens and the like – all within a few hundred yards of the foot of London Bridge.

The reader, then, will agree that Southwark merits a chapter to itself.

We will take our first look at Southwark through the eyes of the incomparable old Stow. He gives a list of the noble houses I have mentioned above, and it is up to our imagination to form a picture of their magnificence, of the power their occupiers exerted, and the extent of the ill-paid servitude which their maintenance demanded. Here, then, are a few of the great houses which stood on the site of the none too salubrious Southwark of today.

Firstly there was the house of the bishop of Winchester, a high-powered ecclesiastic whose diocese directly or indirectly had great influence over Southwark. Stow calls it "his lodging when he cometh to this city". The house was first built in 1107 by William Gifford, bishop of Winchester, on a plot of land attached to the abbey of Bermondsey nearby. This house, says Stow, was a very fair house, well repaired, with a large wharf and landing-place called the Bishop of Winchester's Stairs.

Almost next to it was the "inn or lodging" of the bishop of Rochester, who, however, used it but little, so that it fell into a state of great dilapidation, though it had once been a fine example of the great London houses of the time. Then there was the duke of Suffolk's house, known as Southwark Place;

likewise the houses of the abbot of Hyde (near Winchester), the house of the prior of Lewes, of the abbot of St Augustine and that of the abbot of Battaile. Altogether a nice assortment of "lodgings" for the plump abbots when they came importantly to London. Not all of these houses survived the attentions of the followers of Jack Cade and Wat Tyler and, in particular, the malcontents of Sir Thomas Wyatt who completely sacked the Winchester bishop's house and destroyed his vast library. The other great houses have fallen victims to Time and what we call Progress, though there are still a few of the old Southwark buildings left, such as the George Inn in the Borough High Street to which I refer presently.

Southwark was at one time a righteous irritation to the citizens of London for, despite the religious undercurrents already inferred, it existed as a real rogues' retreat. Being outside the active jurisdiction of the City it offered a perfect "sanctuary" for evil-doers who, having committed their crimes there, simply crossed the river and enjoyed their gains. But this immunity was too good to last. The City (which owned property in Southwark) petitioned the king for the right of its officers to chase up the bad boys in the confines of Southwark itself. This was granted by Edward III, and later by Henry IV, and Southwark eventually became The Bridge Ward Without of the City of London, the "without" signifying that it was not within the City walls or the boundaries appertaining to them.

But the unwholesomeness of parts of Southwark was by no means confined to the thieves and vagabonds we have just mentioned, for the Borough achieved for itself an almost accepted notoriety for its "stews". It is doubtful if the latter-day term, houses of ill-fame, would in any case have been applied to them. They were just stews, and there were more of them than could be found in any other locality in London. They are not mentioned except cursorily in most books about Southwark, but perhaps in these permissive days we may be allowed to quote Stow, who saw them as a part of Southwark. After describing certain other aspects of the Borough he writes:

"Next on the bank was sometime the Bordello, or Stewes, a place so called of certain stewe houses privileged there, for the repair of men and the like women; of which privilege I have read thus: 'In a parliament holden at Westminster, the 8th of Henry II it was ordained by the commons, and confirmed by the king and lords, that divers constitutions should for ever be kept within the lordship or franchise, according to the old customs that had been used there time out of mind; amongst the which these following were some, viz.

'That no stew-holder or his wife should let or stay any single woman to go and come freely as they listed.

That no stew-holder to keep any woman to board, but she to board abroad at her pleasure.

To take no more for the woman's room for the week than fourteen pence.

Not to keep open his doors upon the holidays.

No single woman to be kept against her will that would leave her sin.

No man to be drawn or enticed into any stew-house.

No stew-holder to receive any woman of religion, or any man's wife.

The constables, bailiffs and others, every week to search every stew-house.'

"These and many more orders were to be observed upon great pain and punishment. [Here Stow refers to Wat Tyler's rebels beating up the stews, saying that afterwards the same houses were again confirmed to be continued as before.] Also the said stew-houses were for a season inhibited, and the doors closed up, but it was not long ere the houses were set open again. . . . These allowed stew-houses had signs on their fronts, towards the Thames, not hanging out, but painted on the walls, as a Boar's head, the Cross Keys, the Crane, the Cardinal's Hat, the Bell, etc. I have heard of ancient men of good credit that these single women were forbidden the rites of the church, so long as they continued that sinful life, and were excluded from Christian burial, if they were not reconciled before their death. And therefore there was a plot of ground called the Single Women's Churchyard, appointed for them far from the parish church."

Stow then concludes:

"In the year of Christ 1546, the 37th of Henry VIII, this row of stews in Southwarke was put down by the king's commandment which was proclaimed by the sound of a trumpet, no more to be privileged, but the inhabitants of the same to keep good and honest rule as in other places of this realm."

Southwark, especially in the days of its independence from London, was never short of diversions, most of which were supported by a flow of citizens from across the Thames who were not particularly catered for in the City. Thus, a little to the west of St Saviour's (now the cathedral), there were bear gardens wherein were kept bears and bulls and other animals to be baited. Also close by were a number of kennels in which were kept mastiffs and various dogs, "nourished to bait them". The baiting took place in specially reserved plots of land "scaffolded about for the beholders to stand safe".

Then there was the famous Southwark Fair, held annually in September, and opened by the lord mayor and a retinue of civic dignitaries, including the sword-bearer and the sheriffs, mostly in their scarlet gowns. This fair was a lively occasion and it would need the pencil of a Hogarth to depict what went on there. It originated in 1550 under charter from Edward VI, and, although repeated efforts were made to suppress it, it was not until 1703 or thereabouts that it finally ended. Meanwhile, the fair days (and nights) meant a thronging of London Bridge almost to the point of danger.

Another Southwark attraction for Londoners was the pleasure garden known as the Paris Garden which, apparently, was a forerunner [of the famous Cremorne Gardens at Chelsea a century or so later, though on a smaller scale. The latter, however, seemed to lack the responsibility of the Paris Gardens, for it attracted a lower type of patron; so much so that eventually they were closed on account of disorder along the river bank after the nightly "closing-time". The Paris Garden was of a different order, and was the site of the Paris Garden Theatre. It was one of the most important of the London theatres and ranked with the Globe in Southwark and the Blackfriars, in each of which Shakespeare was a considerable shareholder.

At one time there were five well-known prisons, some with courts attached and under the jurisdiction of London. They were: the Clink, the Comptor, the King's Bench, the Marshalsea and the White Lion. The last, as its name implies, was actually an inn, though not infrequently used as "a common hostelrie for the receipt of travellers". The Clink gave its name to Clink Street, still so called, and it is said that Shakespeare once had a house there. The King's Bench Prison was unique in that it was made occasionally to move its functions to various parts of the country according to where certain judges might be sitting. Thus, the King's Bench Court and Chancery was once removed to York, with the prison attached to it, but the whole lot were eventually moved back to London at the command of Edward III, and the prisoners' "headquarters" returned to the prison in Southwark. It was mainly a debtors' gaol, as was the Comptor. There were various Comptor prisons in London, and it is interesting to note that in the cellars of a Cheapside wine-merchant may be seen, still attached to the walls, the chains which were once used to secure the limbs of prisoners.

But the most interesting prison of all was the Marshalsea which stood opposite Maypole Alley in the Borough High Street. Over a long period it housed a wide miscellany of prisoners, from the high-born (including Bishop Bonner) to felons of the lowest degree and even pirates. It had a court of justice attached to it, which was abolished as late as 1887. Many stories could be told of it. One concerns a certain esquire who killed a sailor in Southwark, on which a number of angered sailors "brought a suit against him in the court of the Marshalsea". Stow, in telling the story, says:

"But when they perceived that court to be so favourable to the murderer, and also the king's warrant for his pardon had been gotten for the murderer they in fury ran to the house wherein the murderer was confined, brake into it, and brought forth the prisoner with the gyves on his legs; they thrust a knife into his heart, and stickt him as if he had been a dog; after this they tied a rope to his gyves, and drew him to the gallows where, when they had hanged him, as though they had done a great act, they caused the trumpets to be sounded before them to their ships, and there in great triumph they spent the rest of the day."

Needless to say, the prison was broken open more than once by the rebels of Kent of whom we have read.

Southwark in its heyday was remarkably served with inns. This was no doubt due to the large number of carts which were driven long distances from the country to bring produce into London, distances which could not be covered both ways in a day, or even two, so that the drivers would put up for the night in the Borough. There were not sufficient inns with stabling on the other side of London Bridge. Many of the Southwark inns had ample stabling, employed ostlers and catered well for "man and his beast". Among the more notable of these were the White Hart, the Queen's Head, the Bull, the George and, of course, the Tabard to which Geoffrey Chaucer gave lasting fame by lodging his "Canterbury Pilgrims" there for the night before sending them on their tale-telling walk towards Canterbury. But you will see no Tabard in Southwark today; there is a public house on its site but it is no Tabard, or anything like it. The old White Hart was the "Hart" at which Jack Cade stayed. Of the other inns I have mentioned above, none remains except the George.

The George, in the Borough High Street (as was the Tabard), is one of the remaining galleried inns in London. It has the usual "coaching" yard, and there remains on one side of the yard a wealth of galleries of carved oak giving access to bedrooms. It was totally burnt down in the Great Fire of Southwark which occurred some ten years after the Great Fire of London. Southwark's private Great Fire as we might say! It was duly rebuilt and much of it remains with us today after 300 years (plate 28). It is within a few hundred yards of the foot of London Bridge and is close to Guy's Hospital, which itself stands near the site of the one-time St Thomas's Hospital which eventually was succeeded by the great hospital of that name near the end of Westminster Bridge.

There seems no need to describe the Great Fire of Southwark, as it followed the pattern of many other fires which occurred in London through the ages. Nevertheless it was a disastrous conflagration and, according to one account, destroyed about 900 houses before it was brought to a halt by the stone walls of St Thomas's Hospital. It was also notable on account of the celebrities who flocked there and flooded the workers with advice. These included the king and queen who came down the Thames to the bridge-foot in their royal barge. Others were the duke of Monmouth, the earl of Craven and the lord mayor who superintended the blowing-up of buildings in a worthy attempt to halt the blaze. According to a report in the *London Gazette* of 29 May 1676 (the year of the fire), the disaster marked the introduction of a new and valuable type of fire-engine, thus: "Whereas his Majesty hath granted letters-patent unto Mr Wharton and Mr Strode, for a certain new invention for quenching of fire, with *leathern* pipes, which carries a great quantity and a continual stream of water, with an extraordinary force, to the top of any house, into any room, passage or alley; being much more useful than any other which hath been invented, as was attested of the Masters of St. Thomas's Hospital and officers of the same parish, as in the late great fire of Southwark, to their great benefit."

Many houses, gabled and picturesque, disappeared in the making of approaches to the new London Bridge which succeeded the six-centuries-old structure begun by Peter de Colechurch and which added so many pages to the history of London.

The Globe Theatre of Will Shakespeare stood near the end of Bankside where now a great brewery sprawls, and there is a notice nearby to proclaim the fact. It was, like the Paris Garden Theatre, a strange structure by modern standards. Each presented an octagonal, flat-topped outward appearance. An amusing story exists about the Globe being burnt to the ground in Shakespeare's day. It is told in a letter written by Sir Henry Wotton to a friend. Wotton was an ambassadorial diplomat, but remains also as a poet, and the verses he wrote to Elizabeth of Bohemia merited, much later, inclusion in Palgrave's *Golden Treasury*, one of the choicest verse anthologies extant.

But to return to his amusing letter about the fire at Southwark's Globe:

"Now, to let matters of state sleep, I will entertain you with what happened this week at the Bankside. The King's players had a new play called 'All is True', representing some principal pieces of the reign of Henry VIII, which was set forth with many extraordinary circumstances of pomp and majesty, even to the matting on the stage, the knights of the Order with their Georges and garters, the guests with their embroidered coats, and the like; sufficient to make greatness very familiar, if not ridiculous. Now King Henry [in the play, of course], making a mask at the Cardinal Wolsey's house, and certain cannons being shot off at his entry, some of the paper or other stuff wherewith one of them was stopped, did light on the thatch where, being thought at first but an idle smoke and their eyes being more attentive to the show, it kindled inwardly, and ran round like a train [of powder], consuming, within less than an hour, the whole house to the very ground. This was the fatal period of that virtuous fabric, wherein nothing did perish but wood and straw and a few forsaken cloaks; only one man had his breeches set on fire, that perhaps had broiled him, if he had not, by the benefit of a provident wit, put it out with bottle ale."

The play, presumably, was Shakespeare's *Henry VIII*, which may have been first called *All is True*, the stage directions of which demanded some form of innocent firearms.

Happily the Globe was rebuilt in the following year. In the end it shared the fate of most London theatres and was closed down by the joyless Commonwealth.

There were a number of interesting industries in Southwark at that time, and many were the London tradesmen who crossed London Bridge to patronise them. These industries were, like the senior Mr Weller's knowledge of London, "extensive and peculiar". There were, says Timbs in his *Curiosities of London* (1855), "rope-walks, tan-pits (tanneries), barge and boat-builders, sawyers and timber merchants; also hat-making, breweries, vinegar-yards and distilleries, glass houses, potteries, and soap and candle works". We could add more. The reference to "glass houses" is interesting, for Southwark was once famous for its stained glass, and made the now precious windows of King's College, Cambridge, in the reign of Henry VIII.

The story of Southwark, from the romantic historian's point of view, seems well touched upon in this cursory account of the Bridge Ward Without. Certainly Southwark is not as it was, but we cannot by any means apply to it the word Ichabod which, as the Old Testament tells us, means "The Glory is Departed". We have still the Cathedral of St Saviour's, with its load of almost ten centuries' history, standing at the very foot of London Bridge, seen daily by the millions of commuters who use London Bridge Station. Except that it stands below road level, it is almost part of the bridge itself.

Southwark Cathedral, as I have mentioned elsewhere, is considered to be the finest ecclesiastical building in London, with the exception of Westminster Abbey, though we could probably add a few more exceptions but not on the cathedral scale. It was founded as a college of sisters by Mary Audery, and was converted by the bishop of Winchester into a college of canons, or priests. It suffered various vicissitudes and eventually became known as the Church of St Mary Overy's or Overie, the name based on *ofer* (bank) and *rie* (river). In view of the situation by the Thames the name is quite understandable. Later the church became St Saviour's, a name taken from the suppressed Abbey of St Saviour in nearby Bermondsey. Its name survives and it is now the Cathedral Church of St Saviour's, having become the seat of a bishopric in 1905.

The Harvard family, as every good American knows, had a close link with Shakespeare in Southwark. John Harvard's father, Robert – a well-to-do "fleshmonger" – was twice married, his first wife falling victim to the plague of Southwark which raged in 1603. His second wife was Katherine Rogers of Stratford-upon-Avon, whom he met while on a visit to Stratford with his friend William Shakespeare whose home town it was. Some accounts say that it was the playright himself who introduced Robert Harvard to the Rogers family (well known in Stratford). John Harvard was a child of this marriage and was baptised in St. Saviour's in 1607, perhaps with Shakespeare at the ceremony.

When Robert Harvard died in a later plague in or about 1625 he left a considerable sum to his two sons, of whom John Harvard was one. This fortune, together with a later legacy from his mother, enabled him, after a Cambridge career, to emigrate to America, there to found what is now the world-famed Harvard University.

9

THE WRITING ON THE WALL

Eventually old age "with its infirmities which no art can cure" crept up on the six-centuries-old bridge, and there were many moves by high authorities to have it replaced. But the Court of Common Council, which governed, and still largely does, the City of London, refused to sanction a new bridge, so that the old one for many years was maintained by continual propping and tinkering, the cost of which grew yearly.

As a safety precaution, however, its houses and shops were begun to be removed in 1757 (plates 8 and 9). This presented a sad sight to Londoners. Gone would be the old familiar houses and shops, gone the needle-makers and print-sellers, and gone the glovers, the dry-salters and the distillers of strong waters; gone too the one-time houses of famous artists and of the priests of St Magnus the Martyr nearby. But the obvious reason for all this was the impending uselessness of the bridge in the face of the steady increase of river shipping as London advanced to its ultimate position in the world, not to mention the growing surge of traffic which squeezed its way between the picturesque buildings on either side. Fond citizens might close their eyes to this, but the writing was on the wall nevertheless.

The processes which led to the "demolitionists" getting their way were a tangle of arguments, deputations, select committees, Parliamentary debates, City wrangles and everything save action. But what eventually brought the matter to a climax – a somewhat premature climax it is true – was the new Thames bridge at Westminster. Hitherto there had been no other structure to compare with London Bridge, but by the time of which we speak there had been completed a fine bridge at

26. Chair fashioned from the once submerged piles of
Peter de Colechurch's bridge. The bridge motif
dominates the work, which is exhibited at Fishmongers' Hall.

27. Statue in elm of Sir William Walworth holding the dagger with which he slew Wat Tyler. Exhibited at Fishmongers' Hall.

28. The George, at Southwark:
the only galleried inn left
in London.

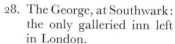

29. A performance of David
Copperfield at the George
at Southwark where Shake-
spearian and Dickensian
plays are frequently staged
in the courtyard.

30. The three arches of Rennie's London Bridge shortly before the new bridge was begun. Tower Bridge is in the background.

31. Commuters crossing London Bridge on their way from London Bridge Station to the City at 9 a.m. The strain of this pedestrian traffic was partly responsible for the decision to build a new bridge.

32. Blocks of granite at the Surrey Docks ready for shipment to Lake Havasu, Arizona.

33 and 34. Stonework from the old bridge (above) and five Roman heads (below) – which once formed part of the façade of a City building – on the first leg of their journey to the Arizona tourist spot where they will be incorporated in the rebuilding of London Bridge.

35. One of a series of granite souvenirs made from Rennie's London Bridge for home and export, especially to America.

36. Mr Harold King, City Engineer (right), greeting the Chairman and President of the McCulloch Oil Corporation, purchasers.

37. The old London Bridge pedestrian walk has been closed and commuters pour across the walk on the new bridge which is wired for heating in frosty weather.

38. London Bridge with the Arizona Desert – not the Thames – flowing beneath it at Lake Havasu City, U.S.A.

Westminster which strongly challenged our old friend. It had taken some ten years to build – from 1738 to 1749 – and had many features which London Bridge lacked, such as width and more practical approaches. It was this that moved the Court of Common Council, and the City generally, to agree that a new bridge must be eventually built. But even then it was sixty years before the matter was tackled in earnest. Meanwhile much money was spent and scores of lives lost in waterway accidents against the piers and sterlings of the bridge. An acid comment was made at the time that "had an Alderman or a turtle been lost there, the nuisance would long have been removed".

However, by 1754 the matter took a definite turn, and we are told by the *Public Advertiser* of that period that the Court of Common Council took into consideration a motion for the construction of a new bridge between London and Southwark but, after a debate of four hours, the motion was withdrawn and a committee appointed to consider in what way the bridge might be restored. Their report was favourable to restoration, stating that the foundations of the bridge were in good order, but recommending the pulling down of the houses on the bridge and those in the narrow streets which formed the immediate approaches to the structure. There was also the proposition that two of the arches should be removed, and one wide central arch substituted. This would create a safer and more commodious waterway than that which previously rushed, almost torrentially at times, through the narrow arches.*

The bridge, by this time, had reached a sorry state, especially as viewed from the walks and wharves immediately below it. Walter Harrison, a well-known historian of the time, thus described this non-artistic prospect of the bridge:

"On the outer part of the Bridge, on the East side, the view from the wharfs and quays was exceedingly disagreeable. Nineteen disproportioned arches, the sterlings increased to an amazing size by frequent repairs, supported the street above. These arches were of very different sizes, and several that were low and narrow were placed between others that were broad and lofty. The back part of the houses next the Thames had neither beauty nor uniformity; the line being broken by a great

* See "Shooting the Bridge" in Miscellany at the end of the book

number of closets that projected from the buildings and hung
over the sterlings. This deformity was greatly increased by the
houses projecting farther over it than the others; by which
means the tops of almost all the arches, except those that were
nearest, were concealed from the view of the passengers on the
quays, and made the Bridge look like a multitude of rude piers,
with only an arch or two at the ends, and the rest, consisting of
beams, extending from the flat tops of the piers, without any
other arches, quite across the river."

Maybe Harrison was unduly critical, for Norden described
the bridge in the time of Elizabeth in enthusiastic terms. He
even remarked that some of the houses had platform roofs with
pretty little gardens and arbours. But, of course, much had
happened to the bridge since Elizabeth's day, for many of the
houses were burned or blown down more than once and rebuilt.
So perhaps Harrison was not far off the mark.

Following the report mentioned above the restorations were
at last put in hand, when it was deemed necessary to erect a
temporary wooden bridge to perform the functions of the old
one during the alterations. This sounds uneventful, yet the
temporary bridge was due to provide as great a sensation as
most which had attended the old one during its long history.
It provided, too, a mystery which has never been satisfactorily
solved; that is to say, how came it about that on an April night
in 1758 the temporary bridge caught fire and was reduced to a
mass of charcoal-covered beams, most of which had fallen into
the river by noon of the following day? (Plate 10.)

The lord mayor and other dignitaries were quickly at the
scene, but there was nothing they could do except hold what
must have been panic-stricken discussions, at one of which it
was decided that the fire was not accidental but had been
deliberately caused by man's hands. There was no doubt about
the seriousness of the conflagration, for there was now no communication, in the accepted sense, between the City and
Southwark, except by ferries which were augmented at the
instigation of the lord mayor. Another effect of the fire was to
destroy the "troughs" which carried water to Southwark from
the water-works on the old bridge.*

* Described in the Miscellany

The situation demanded a sharp inquiry into the cause of the fire, an immediate outcome of which was the issuing of a king's pardon to all acquainted with the incendiarism "excepting the person who actually set the bridge on fire", with a reward of £200 from the Corporation of London to anyone who could bring the culprit to book. Then came an examination of the various pieces of evidence of somewhat sketchy credulity. Thus several watchmen of the City and Southwark told that just previously to the outbreak they noticed lights moving about among the under-structure of the bridge. Other evidence was that several drunken persons were seen crossing the bridge by the light of torches which, after a bout of horseplay, were thrown over the palings. Then flames broke out and increased in intensity till the whole bridge was on fire. Next, a watchman deposed that a person was seen rowing round the base of the bridge and occasionally flashing a "lanthorn", and that shortly afterwards the bridge was seen to be in flames. But the most reliable witness seems to have been a Mrs Dennis who at a relevant time was in the Dyers' Hall on the west side of Dowgate Hill near where Cannon Street Station now stands. She made her deposition before the lord mayor thus:

"About ten o'clock on the night of the fire she looked out of a door [at the Dyers' Hall] and saw a lanthorn in the Chapel pier. Soon after she saw another, and then, losing sight of both, there presently appeared three in the same place. At first she thought that some vessel was at the Bridge, but the appearance of the second light showed her that they were between the woodwork of the great pier; and when the three lanthorns were visible together, she observed that one was held up and another down towards the timbers. These lights she imagined to proceed from workmen, but in a short time she saw a small flame burst out on the same spot, which was damped, and then brake out again, and, after being damped a second time, blazed very fiercely: upon which the deponent went to the next wharf, and gave notice that London Bridge was on fire."

Later, several other people testified to having seen the same unusual sight.

Meanwhile, according to the *Chronicles*, rumours were flying around with a speed true to type. The lower orders, we are told,

accused the watermen and lightermen (to whom London
Bridge was no friend!); another class attributed the fire to those
who supported the idea of a new bridge altogether. Others
attributed the fire to some deep-laid plot not discernible on the
surface. Certainly the temporary bridge was "the object of
imprecations from the common people", who might be tempted
to fire it from the inconveniences which they experienced upon
it; as in winter it was so excessively dirty, that some supposed
the Committee had contrived it so to increase the toll, by
obliging all passengers to cross it in carriages; whilst in dry
weather it was no less incommoded by dust. Some said this:
some said that. But no one said anything, not even Mrs Dennis,
definitely to pin the fire down to incendiarism. Indeed there
were various arguments put forward to prove the reverse. At
least one of these was interesting. In such a mixture of wood and
stone, it was said, a heap of quicklime on the sterlings, acci-
dentally wetted by the tide, might kindle any adjoining (dry)
woodwork. Another theory was that it was usual for servants
on coaches, with flambeaux in their hands, to extinguish them
by striking them on the rear wheels of the coach, and that one
may have struck his flambeau on the pallisades of the bridge
itself, the flaming wax of which, dropping into some joint, might
have set the timber alight.

Mention of flambeaux recalls the paucity of lighting in which
street progression was made even in those comparatively later
days. These flambeaux were a somewhat larger type of link-
lights and were mainly used on carriages. They were long
hollow torches filled with tow soaked in pitch and tallow and
burned furiously if not very brightly. The same could be said
of link-lights used throughout London by pedestrians going to
their homes at night. They were usually carried by link-boys
who, for a small fee, would guide people to their doors, whereupon the links would be extinguished in a funnel-shaped link
extinguisher which was fixed on the outside of many houses.
Examples of this may still be discovered in London, but the best
are probably those on the three Wren houses in Amen Court
near St Paul's Cathedral where they are affixed by ornate
wrought iron work.

The cause of the fire was never established, but one fact does
emerge from the episode, and that is the alacrity with which the

City Corporation erected a new bridge. At least 500 workmen were immediately set to work upon the task. They worked whole-heartedly, even to the extent of working on the Sabbaths following the catastrophe. The astonishing result was that within a month of the fire a new temporary bridge came into being, fully capable of dealing with the amount of traffic which had passed over before. There is something agreeable in looking back on that accomplishment, unhampered by strikes, go-slows, working-to-rule and similar impediments not unknown in like circumstances today. As a precaution against any such disaster occurring again it was ordered "that two men, well armed, should be placed every night, from sun-set to sun-rise, in a gallery erected from end to end of the temporary bridge, just beneath the centre of the works, with lamps lighted, and a bell to alarm the neighbourhood in case of an attack". As an extra precaution the lord mayor ordered that no coaches or foot-passengers should carry lighted torches over the new structure.

Eventually the repairs and alterations to the old bridge were completed, but there was still trouble in store for our old friend. A new large central arch was constructed at the expense of two smaller ones, and a more navigable waterway thus created. The operation, however, disturbed both the bed of the river and the adjacent piers. There was danger all around. It was decided to consult the eminent engineer John Smeaton, of Leeds, who came down post-haste (literally) from Yorkshire. (Smeaton was famous in his day, his most noteworthy accomplishment being the building of the third Eddystone lighthouse, the first and second (of timber) having been destroyed by hurricane and fire respectively.) Smeaton made an examination and pronounced the bridge to be in immediate danger. Happily several of the old City gates had recently been demolished, and the stones sold to various builders. (Three of the gates were Ludgate, Cripplegate and Aldgate.) The stones of at least one of these were retrieved and hurried to the bridge, there to be flung into the Thames round the piers and sterlings. And this, one understands, averted what might have been yet another cataclysmic episode in the history of Peter de Colechurch's London Bridge.

There was still to come in the bridge's lifetime another great frost early in 1814, but, as it followed the pattern of the frosts mentioned in a previous chapter, we will not dwell upon it.

There was the usual jolly fair on the ice and, when the thaw came, the usual blocking of the smaller arches of the bridge by enormous, thick slabs of ice. The effects of this frost were unusually important in as much as they called for a renewal of the demand for an entirely new bridge. Here then is an extract from the *Chronicles of London Bridge* dealing with the "Reports and Evidences" of inspections and inquiries made at the time:

"The craft, etc., on the River having increased one-third within the last 20 years, the water-way at London Bridge was no longer sufficient for them; since the larger loaded barges, in general, went through the great arch, which they could pass only for about six hours out of 24, or the first three after high water. On this account there was considerable danger at the flood-tide, because the loaded barges, then crowding to get through, were all equally impelled to the same point; and thus very frequently damaged, sunk or locked together in the Arch. Another cause of great danger was the getting on a sterling when the water had covered it only enough to prevent it being visible; for if a barge passed over it but a few feet or even inches, and stopped upon not finding enough water, if it got on the edge, as the water sank it fell over; or, if in the middle, was detained there until the next tide. This evil, too, was stated to be continually increasing, from the constant repairs of the sterlings which considerably extended their size."

We will now pass on to the beginning of the nineteenth century, when a somewhat drastic report came: "The Third Report from The Select Committee upon the Improvement of the Port of London, 1800", in which it was definitely stated, "the great, continual and ineffectual expenses of the old Bridge, its irremediable insecurity, and the dangers of its navigation", had induced the Committee to collect information and provide designs for the building of a new one.

In due course a selection of architect-engineers were invited to submit designs, etc., for the new bridge. They included:

MR RALPH DODD, who proposed a stone bridge of six arches with a centre one of iron having a height of 100 feet, the bridge to be erected on the foundations of the old one. This bridge (and a second one, the plans for which he submitted) was to be "adorned with an entablature and balustrated, statues, sculptures and Corinthian pillars".

MR SAMUEL WYATT suggested, by means of a model without any designs, a bridge wholly of cast iron.

MR THOMAS WILSON (architect of the famous bridge at Bishop's Wearmouth, near Sunderland), proposed a bridge of cast iron with piers of granite. This bridge was to be of generous proportions and for a time seemed to be the favourite choice.

MR ROBERT MYLNE proposed a bridge of five arches, directed towards the Monument, which was to form the centre of a square, and to terminate at its southern end in a new road into Kent.

Three further iron bridges were suggested by THOMAS TELFORD and an associate. The mention of Telford in relation to iron bridges is of special interest to us today. A Scotsman, he was the leading civil engineer of his time, and was responsible for a hundred bridges in that country, as well as for the Caledonian Canal. He settled in London and became the surveyor of public works in Shropshire. In England he built various bridges, also several famous roads such as the Shrewsbury–Holyhead road. The point of interest today, however, is that the vast new town at Dawley in Shropshire, to become an overspill for Birmingham and neighbourhood, has already been given the name of "Telford". This new town will be a neighbour of Coalbrookdale and Ironbridge on the Severn; at the latter little place was erected the first iron bridge in the world, made at Coalbrookdale in 1779. This bridge, a graceful single span of $100\frac{1}{2}$ feet, gave its name to the little town and still stands there today in the steep, verdant Severn Valley (plate 12).

It is of further interest to note that the committee at one time considered making the new London Bridge to be a single-arch iron bridge, after discussions with Telford. They even sent a questionnaire to experts up and down the country. These included the astronomer royal, the inspector of naval works of the Admiralty and William Reynolds of "Colebrook-Dale". But, as we may read, "it was probably the very great diversity of sentiment prevailing in the answers that caused this design to be ultimately abandoned". So the Thames did not get its single-arch bridge of iron. Nor did Telford get the job.

The design of John Rennie was eventually adopted. Rennie

was one of the greatest civil engineers of his time, and examples of his genius could and can be found in various parts of the country. He was responsible for numerous canals, including the Kennet and Avon and the Rochdale, whilst his work on different docks is not to be forgotten; these included the docks at Hull, Chatham and Sheerness. But his masterpiece was the early Waterloo Bridge, already built at the time of which we are speaking. (It was completed in 1817 and was opened on the second anniversary of the battle of Waterloo.)

Rennie did not live to see his design for London Bridge take shape, for he died in 1821, leaving two sons, one of them being George, a ship-builder of repute, and the other John, who carried on the work of London Bridge and received a knighthood. The name of Sir John Rennie is indissolubly connected with the bridge, though the design emanated from his father.

It is worth mentioning that in 1823 Royal Assent (of George IV) was granted to "An Act for the Rebuilding of London Bridge, and for making suitable approaches thereto". Among the "terms of reference" were "to take down and sell the old Bridge, either leaving it till the completion of the new one, or erecting a temporary structure before removing it; to build a new edifice of Granite, either on the present site, or within 180 feet westward, with convenient approaches, according to the designs of John Rennie, Esq. . . ."

It was decided to retain the old bridge until the new one was built, the site of the latter being some 100 feet upstream. The new bridge was to consist of five elliptical arches, whereas the arches of the old one were somewhat gothic in form. This shape is not always apparent in many old engravings, an aberration due perhaps to artistic licence, to which we might also attribute the inability of many artists, past and present, to portray the dome of St Paul's exactly as it is; it may need a fine eye to discern where they go wrong, but go wrong they often do!

The foundation stone of the new bridge was laid in 1825, and the completed structure opened on 1 August 1831.

———∘⊚∘———

CROWDED HOURS

If ancient bridges have consciousness – and one is tempted to believe they have! – then Peter de Colechurch's venerable structure must have grieved on 15 June 1825 at the high jinks of the ungrateful Londoners at the laying of the foundation stone of the Rennies' new bridge. This occasion, like the royal opening some seven years later, was accompanied by the height of civic ceremony, to read of which, in these less colourful days, is to invite nostalgia, for since then pageantry and the Thames have parted company.

So let us take a look at that June day which moved the folk of London and Southwark almost to hysteria. Excitement had mounted high when it became known that the enormous muddle of scaffolding was at last to reveal something tangible in the way of a new bridge. The first sign that something significant was in the offing was the work on the construction of the great coffer dam in which the stone-laying ceremony was to take place beneath the surface level of the Thames. A coffer dam is not easy to describe in non-technical language, but it may be called, according to one reference book, "a water-tight barricade formed round an area which is to be freed from water so as to permit excavation of construction of foundations". In this case the coffer dam was built on an unprecedented scale so that there was a vast watertight compartment to accommodate the hundreds of people who were to attend the great ceremony. The stone was to be laid on the "floor" of the coffer dam which was 45 feet below high water mark (plate 14). The first pile of the new bridge had been driven on 15 March, and a good deal of excavation had been made at the site, which was some 30 yards upstream from the old bridge. During this excavation a number of interesting finds were brought to light. These included, according to Timbs' *Curiosities of London*, brass and copper coins of Augustus, Vespasian and other Roman emperors, Venetian tokens, Nuremberg counters and a few tradesmen's tokens; brass and silver rings and buckles, ancient iron keys and silver spoons, remains of an engraved gilt dagger, an iron spear-head and a fine bronze lamp (head of Bacchus) and a small silver figure of Harpocrates. (Harpocrates was an Egyptian deity worshipped by the Greeks and Romans.) It is a choice little figure and shows the god with his fingers to his lips, signifying that he was the god of silence. At his feet are a dog, an owl and a tortoise, though precisely what they signify I have not discovered. This little statue – it is only $2\frac{1}{2}$ inches tall – was presented at the time to the British Museum.

The coffer dam (plate 13) was built adjacent to the fourth arch at the Southwark end of the old bridge and was connected to it by an elaborate passage and a flight of steps which were to act as the grand entrance to the scene of the ceremony, by the time of which the walls and floors of passage and steps were covered with crimson cloth, the walls also being draped with large flags of Britain and the Empire. Meanwhile notices had begun to appear about the City and Southwark, as follows:

LONDON BRIDGE. MANSION HOUSE, 23rd May, 1825
The Committee for the Rebuilding the new London Bridge having appointed Wednesday, the 15th day of June next, for laying the First Stone of the New Bridge, Notice is hereby given, that the Foot and Carriageway over the present Bridge will be stopped on that day from Eleven o'clock in the Forenoon until four o'clock in the Afternoon.
By the Order of the Right Honourable the Lord Mayor,
FRANCIS HOBLER
N.B. – *Southwark Bridge will be open free of Toll during the above hours.*

As may be imagined, the appearance of this notice greatly increased the excitement which already prevailed. Crowds gathered daily on the old bridge to watch the comings and goings of men and materials to the somewhat mysterious coffer dam. Of special interest was a hugh steam engine with a tall funnel, for use in extracting water from the dam. Meanwhile flagstaffs had begun to appear on nearly every eminence where one could be put, in preparation for the greatest display of flags ever seen in London. Scaffolds for letting purposes appeared with astonishing rapidity, and notices were displayed giving the seating charges, which varied from 2s. 6d. to 15s. according to what could be seen from the various vantage points.

Excitement followed excitement and continued to mount when it became known that the lord mayor was to be accompanied by the duke of York, and again when it was announced that the Monument was to be illuminated, on the night of the Day, by *portable gas*. It must be remembered that gas, as a public illuminant, was then in its infancy. But the illumination of the Monument turned out to be not quite the success anticipated. Gas lights (of the naked variety in those days) were placed at suitable intervals in the loopholes of the column so that they gave the impression of the Monument being wreathed in flames. Unfortunately a summer breeze sprang up and blew out a number of the lights which somewhat destroyed the illusion.

The duke of York was the second son of George III (the first son becoming George IV). He became commander-in-chief of the army and was in charge of several unfortunate expeditions to the Continent. He was immortalised in the rhyme:

> *The brave old Duke of York*
> *He had ten thousand men,*
> *He marched them up to the top of a hill*
> *And he marched them down again.*
> *And when they were up, they were up;*
> *And when they were down, they were down;*
> *And when they were half-way up*
> *They were neither up nor down.*

He was ultimately relieved of his overseas command by the king at the insistence of Prime Minister Pitt, though he continued as a fairly able army administrator at home.

Then came the Day itself.

"A finer and more freshly breathing air was never abroad than that which cooled the atmosphere and blew out the gaily-coloured flags around old London Bridge on the morning of June 15th. At a very early hour workmen began erecting the barriers which were double and some distance apart. Across the whole space of Fish Street Hill, from Upper and Lower Thames Street, and again at Tooley Street [on the Southwark side] there stretched wide wooden railings, having a moveable bar at each pavement, with an opening wide enough for one person only; whilst the centre of the Street [i.e. the old bridge] was divided with posts and bars, allowing carriages to pass between them, but only in single lines. . . . So long as the barriers continued open, the old Bridge was crowded with gazers; who were especially collected opposite that part of the parapet which was to form the grand entrance to the Coffer-Dam; while on the roofs of the houses and other buildings in the vicinity, were platforms of seats, and awnings preparing, which were afterwards crowded with spectators; as well as the Monument, St Magnus' Church, the towers of St Mary Overie, and St Olave and Fishmongers' Hall, and the Patent Shot Works."

Long before the hour of closing the old bridge the river presented a colourful scene. Apart from the flags already mentioned we now had a multitude of vessels, most of them sporting flags of one sort or another. Further, many of the pleasure boats – and there were many of them swarming around – had bands aboard, and the resultant cacophony is not difficult to imagine. The old bridge, so stolid over its centuries, had truly let its hair down. But the real excitement was yet to come.

The committee responsible for the new bridge had full reason to be proud. It comprised, under the lord mayor, all the aldermen and various big-wigs of the City, including representatives of all the wards of the City, most of which bear the same names today – Candlewick, Aldersgate Within (and Without), Farringdon likewise, Cordwainers, Bread Street, Portsoken, Cheap, Bridge, Cripplegate and so on. To these members was granted the right to issue tickets of admission to the coffer dam. These were worded as shown on the next page.

This ticket admitted its holder to the coffer dam galleries only; there was another ticket, slightly more elegant, for the *élite* which allowed entry to the platforms. The difference between these two viewing points can be seen in our illustration of the suspended foundation stone (plate 14).

Admit the Bearer
To Witness the Ceremony of Laying
THE FIRST STONE
of the
New London Bridge
On Wednesday, the 15th Day of June, 1825
(Signed) HENRY WOODTHORPE, Junr.,
Clerk of the Committee.

N.B. *The Access is from the Present Bridge and the time of Admission will be between the hours of Twelve and Two.*

The time spent waiting for the opening hour was enlivened by hearty band music played by the Artillery Company and the Horse Guards who were accommodated in special seats near the entrance to the dam. Meanwhile the spectators could beguile themselves with a variety of refreshments which even included champagne, the latter, presumably, for the privileged few. Then, at four o'clock, came the shattering roar of the signal-gun which announced that the lord mayor's procession, including the duke of York, was on the point of leaving Guildhall. It cannot be boring to take a look at the composition of this procession, so an abbreviated list of its components in order is shown on the next page.

Such then was the procession which sparked off the resounding signal-gun to tell the City the great hour had arrived. The route from Guildhall to the bridge was festooned with bunting and draped with banners, while every window was packed with cheering onlookers.

As the procession came to a stop on old London Bridge, opposite the gaudy entrance to the coffer dam, the scene was one of brilliant colour, with scarlet predominating, supplied by the civic robes of the aldermen and others, not to speak of the regalia of the lord mayor himself. To all this His Royal Highness the duke of York supplied a restrained contrast. He wore, we are told, a plain blue coat, "with the Garter round his knee, and the star of the Order upon his breast".

A division of the Artillery Company
A Band of Music
The Junior City Marshal on Horseback
Barge Masters
City Watermen with Colours
Model of Bridge borne by Labourers etc.
Architect and Engineer, John Rennie, F.R.S.
High Bailiff of the Borough of Southwark
Clerk of the Peace of the City
The Remembrancer
Judges of the Sheriff's Court
Members of Parliament, Visitors
Sir Humphrey Davy, President Royal Society
The two Sheriffs
The Recorder of London
Privy Councillors and Peers, Visitors
Music and Colours with the Court of the
Lord Mayor's Company, the Goldsmiths
The Senior City Marshall on Horseback
The Lord Mayor in his State Carriage
Accompanied by His Royal Highness the
DUKE OF YORK
The remainder of the Artillery Company as a
Guard of Honour to the Lord Mayor

"The Lord Mayor and his Royal Highness having arrived at the state chair, amid the waving of handkerchiefs and the loudest cheers, and both of them having declined the seat of honour, they remained standing during the whole of the ceremony; which was then commenced by the Ward schools and the visitors singing *God Save the King* verse and chorus, in which the Duke also joined with great enthusiasm. The Lord Mayor then moved towards the eastern end of the Platform, in the centre of the Coffer Dam floor, where there was a small stage covered with crimson cloth, attended by four members of the Bridge Committee, bearing the bottle for the coins, an inscription incrusted in glass, the level, and the splendid silver-gilt Trowel for laying the First Stone."

This trowel was evidently a considerable implement, being about a foot long and five inches wide, beautifully designed and reposing in a leather casket lined with white silk. On one face was engraved a reclining figure of Father Thames with the City Arms and supporters beneath it, while on the reverse side was an inscription suitably spaced in "grave-stone" style which, put in plain style, was as follows:

"This Trowel was used in the laying of THE FIRST STONE of the NEW LONDON BRIDGE on the 15th day of June, 1825, in the sixth year of the reign of His Most Gracious Majesty GEORGE THE FOURTH, by the Right Honourable JOHN GARRATT, Lord Mayor of the City of London who was born in the Ward in which the Bridge is situated on the 15th day of December, 1786; elected a Member of the Common Council for that Ward, on the 3rd day of August, 1809. Alderman thereof on the 10th day of March, 1821; and Sheriff of London and Middlesex on the 24th day of June following."

As part of the ceremony Mr John Rennie (he was not knighted until later) displayed before the lord mayor and the duke of York an architectural drawing showing what the bridge would be like when completed. Then came the City chamberlain with a purse containing a set of new coins of the realm; these were placed in a cut-glass bottle for depositing in the hollow which was to receive the lowered foundation stone. Next came the town clerk with the brass depositum plate, also to be placed in the hollow and inscribed with a Latin inscription composed by the master of Oriel College, Oxford. This also was inscribed in "grave-stone" style and was of such interest that I give here a free translation:

"The free course of the river being obstructed by the numerous piers of the ancient bridge, and the passage of boats and vessels through the narrow channels being often attended with danger and loss of life by reason of the force and rapidity of the current, the CITY OF LONDON, desirous of providing a remedy for this evil, and at the same time consulting the convenience of commerce in this vast emporium of all nations, under the sanction and with the liberal aid of Parliament, resolved to erect a bridge upon a foundation altogether new, with arches of a wider span, and of a character corresponding to the dignity and importance of this Royal city; Nor does any other time seem to be more suitable for such an undertaking than when, in a period of universal peace, THE BRITISH EMPIRE flourishing in glory, wealth, population and domestic union, is governed by a Prince, the patron and encourager of the arts, under whose auspices the metropolis has been daily advancing in elegance and splendour.

"The first stone of this bridge was laid by John Garratt, Esquire, Lord Mayor, on the 15th day of June, in the sixth year of King George the Fourth, and in the year of Our Lord, 1825.

"JOHN RENNIE, F.R.S., Architect"

There seems more than a hint of sycophancy in this inscription. The Prince was none other than George IV who was thoroughly disliked by his subjects. Indeed his "patronage of the arts" was about the best thing that could be said of him. He behaved disgracefully to his wife who became Queen Caroline on his accession, despite a bill which he inspired, but which was rejected by Parliament, to deprive her of her royal position. Meanwhile he had a long string of mistresses which included Mary Robinson, the actress, Lady Jersey, Lady Hertford and, of course, the celebrated Mrs FitzHerbert. Moreover, the country had to foot the bill for his addiction to gaming and debauchery.

This inscription was elegantly printed and a copy given to all present in the coffer dam.

Next the trowel was handed to the lord mayor, and a eulogistic address spoken to him by the chairman of the Bridge Committee, whereupon the lord mayor turned to the duke of York and addressed him at length, saying, among many other things, that he offered up a fervent prayer that "in executing this great work there would occur no calamity". As it happened no fewer than forty men were to lose their lives, partly owing to the fact that the old narrow-arched bridge stood almost alongside the new one, causing the currents to race.

Presently the great foundation stone was lowered into place – it weighed four tons and was of Aberdeen granite – and the lord mayor advanced to play his part. He gave a few symbolic taps on the stone with a mallet, and carefully applied his spirit-level to the surface, after which the masons got busy with their mortar which only masons know how to do.

No sooner had the stone been "well and truly laid", than there was an outburst of salutes from the Artillery Company present and a reciprocal banging of guns from one of the breweries on the Southwark side of the river. Then, from around, burst out the full-throated strains of the "National Anthem" with brass-band accompaniment, for perhaps the sixth time during the proceedings. The "National Anthem" evidently meant more then than it does now, for it was sung in its entirety. We were at peace at the time, but possible enemies were not overlooked, as witness our plea to the Almighty to "confound their politics, frustrate their knavish tricks".

This was the signal that the day's events were over so far as the coffer dam was concerned. Municipal festivities, however, did not end here, for the lord mayor gave a great banquet at the Mansion House to all the members of his procession, with the exception of the duke of York who had to attend a royal function in the evening. This banquet was notable in as much as more people were entertained than had ever before been in "the Lord Mayor's House". In the Egyptian Hall alone nearly a thousand guests sat down to "Turtle soup, Venison, Champagne, Claret and every other luxury".

Not until 1831 was the Thames at London Bridge again to enjoy such uninhibited rejoicing. That was the year when, the new bridge being completed, it was officially opened by William IV and Queen Adelaide. The scene we have just described could scarcely have been excelled, yet to some extent it was, for the king and queen decided to come down the river in the state barge in procession with other barges, all bedecked with flags and bunting. From the time they embarked from the steps at Somerset House until they reached London Bridge they passed through hordes of decorated craft on either side of the river. After that the occasion followed the pattern of the stone-laying ceremony just described – with the exception that a banquet was held on the bridge itself, a section of which had been covered by an elaborately coloured awning (plates 19 and 20). The awning covered nearly half the bridge and beneath it there sat down to dine some two thousand people, all noteworthy in their own way. At the head of the main table sat King William IV and his consort, Queen Adelaide, with the lord mayor and other City dignitaries close by. It is good to think that our recent London Bridge, which ended its career more or less as a bus route, began it with this "one crowded hour of glorious life" (plate 21).

———⚬⊙⚬———

II

LONDON'S LATEST BRIDGE

Today we are accustoming ourselves to the newest London Bridge. Of its likely permanence we cannot speak, and in this we are reminded of the words of a City historian, H. L. Craik, who in 1851 thus spoke of the then comparatively new Rennies' bridge:

"It is needless to say that the new London Bridge, bestriding the broad river with its five elliptical arches, is a far more magnificent, and in every way more perfect work, than Peter de Colechurch's structure ever was in its best days; and, looking there, in its firm and massive strength, as if it might last a thousand years, it is to the imagination, if we may so speak, as expressive and impressive a monument of the far future as the old bridge was of the past."

Actually it did not work out like that. The difference between the life-spans of the two bridges was that which lies between six and a half centuries and 150 years!

The completion of the Rennies' bridge was not without its alarms, for soon after its opening to traffic it was discovered to be slightly sinking from its true level. The extent of the sinking was but at the rate of one inch in every eight years, but this was enough to call for a watchful eye being kept upon it. The sinking was not due to any constructional error on the part of the Rennies, father and son, but to a lack of understanding of London's sub-soil.

From that point onwards the weight of traffic on the bridge steadily increased, so that eventually about 50,000 pedestrians crossed it daily (plate 31), and a proposal was made a few years ago to widen the bridge to 90 feet as against the existing 65 feet. This, it was assumed, would cope with the ever-increasing burden of traffic, both pedestrian and vehicular, but it was decided that the foundations would not stand up to modern demands. Then came the tentative decision to build an entirely new bridge, and soil experts from the University of London were called in. They too were in favour of a new bridge; indeed they doubted if the Rennie bridge could stand up much longer. And so it came to be.

The new London Bridge, as everyone knows by now, is a structure of outstanding grace, with only three arches, the centre span being 340 feet and the side spans 260 feet. It is interesting to note that Peter de Colechurch's bridge, as first built, had twenty arches, and Sir John Rennie's structure five, so that the present bridge has reached a new "low" in arches! The reinforced concrete is of a special quality to retain its pearl-grey colour which lends itself to the floodlighting which has been installed on a "concealed" plan.

The construction of the new bridge, when completed, will have been a triumph of expediency, having been erected with an absolute minimum of disturbance of the great volume of vehicular and pedestrian traffic daily across the Thames. This was achieved by constructing the new bridge on either side of the old one. The width of the new bridge is 105 feet – a vast improvement on the breadth of Rennie's bridge.

The cost of the new bridge has been £4½ million, and it is gratifying to know that this cost is being met by the Bridge House Estates Fund, so that there is no charge on the City rates, or on the National Exchequer. It may be mentioned that the Bridge House Estates Trust pays for the maintenance of London City's three other bridges – Tower, Southwark and Blackfriars – the Corporation being the trustee of the Bridge House Estates. The latter has developed over the centuries, beginning with profit rentals from the houses which stood on the bridge between 1200 and 1750.

In regard to the new bridge we are met with several interesting facts. We learn that a covered way on each side of the structure was dropped as providing a free and comfortable rendezvous for layabouts and other irresponsible gentry; not that the earlier bridges lacked the attention of undesirables.

Another suggestion which was dismissed was that there should be blocks of flats on the new bridge, thus continuing the old tradition, but problems of modern sanitation presented themselves. There has been one innovation, however, for which users of the bridge must be grateful, particularly the commuters to and from London Bridge Station, and that is the heating of both road and footways in severe weather. The previous bridge's surface was susceptible to icing which gave excitement to many and disablement to quite a few.

The story of how the previous bridge (or much of it) comes to be at Lake Havasu, Arizona, has frequently been told, but a brief recapitulation, worded by the city engineer of the Corporation of London (Mr Harold K. King, C.B.E., C.ENG., F.I.C.E., F.I.MUN.E., etc.), under whose direction the new bridge has been designed and constructed, does not come amiss; particularly as it was Mr King who was asked by the Corporation to sell the bridge (plate 36).

"It must be indeed a very rare experience for a Municipal Engineer to be instructed to sell one of the Authority's bridges, and when this happened I looked back in vain over some thirty years of Municipal experience for guidance or help in this new assignment. The uniqueness of the task, however, soon provided me with a vista of new interest that quickly developed into a fascinating and absorbing one, in its world-wide application. . . .

"A somewhat surprising erroneous – and widely held – impression which had to be corrected throughout was that London Bridge was Tower Bridge – despite the fact that historically a London Bridge has been in existence since the first century, whilst Tower Bridge is only seventy-four years old. I was often quizzed as to why anyone should wish to buy London Bridge – and I think the best answer is one given me by an American – 'that any other bridge is not worth a dime – but London Bridge is something worth bidding for'.

"Promotion was launched by the preparation of an attractive coloured brochure, prepared on a dual basis – as a Form of Tender, and as a historical record for sale to the general public. Copies were sent to British Consulates and Embassies throughout the world and as a result of this distribution were forwarded to the majority of cities in the United States of America. Within a short time over 500 copies were distributed, 10 per cent of which were in reply to requests for tender forms, the remainder merely desiring a copy of the publication. These fifty enquiries came from far and near, from Korea, the United States, Canada, Australia, Spain, France and Switzerland, as well as from this country. Three out of every four were from the United States, and of these the cities from which the largest number came were New York and Los Angeles.

"The tender form stated that a sealed bid for 10,000 tons of elevational granite should be forwarded to the Corporation by the 29th March 1968. However, some six weeks before the closing date it was clear that, in view of the unusualness of the enquiry, personal contact with prospective tenderers was necessary in order that discussions could take place on structural details and availability for re-use. The Corporation decided to send a deputation comprising Mr Luckin, a member of the Bridge House Estates Committee, and myself to spend a week in New York and a similar period in Los Angeles."

A hectic time then ensued for Mr King and Mr Luckin, including a flying visit to Washington to see the British Ambassador there. Then came a series of radio and television appearances at varying hours of the day and night – which is the American way. The upshot of all this was that after a great deal of tough negotiating Mr King returned to London where it was decided to accept the tender of the McCulloch Oil Corporation in the sum of $2,460,000. It has been said that the transportation costs to the McCulloch Corporation will not fall far short of half that figure.

Here is a word from Mr Harold K. King, the city engineer. It refers to a television interview in the N.B.C. "Today" programme at the somewhat alarming hour of 7.15 a.m.:

"After a general discussion with Mrs Aline Saarinan, the interviewer, widow of a well-known architect and who was herself competent to assess the technical problems involved, I was asked if souvenir stones would be available to those who could not afford to bid for the elevational granite, and in replying 'yes', on application to myself and whilst in America c/o the British Information Service, New York, that department received 750 letter requests within 48 hours."

The first application for a piece of the old bridge came from a fifteen-year-old girl named Elizabeth Galaviz and she had the pleasure of receiving her souvenir personally at the hands of Mr Harold King, duly inscribed with her name and set on a small pedestal.

Mr King, despite his responsibilities as chief engineer to the Corporation of London City, and as designer and director of the new London Bridge, must have felt a sense of composure when his hectic visit to the U.S.A. came to an end. Here he tells us of the last stage in "selling London Bridge":

"We returned to London five days before the final date for receipt of tenders with the hope that our visit and the tough negotiating sessions we had experienced had been fruitful. The opening of the tenders was an exciting moment, and I was very pleased and satisfied when the tender accepted by the Bridge House Estates Committee in the sum of $2,460,000 was the sum submitted by the Company who in my opinion had the best scheme of re-use. This Company, the McCulloch Oil Corporation, whose proposed bridge site in Arizona we had visited during our stay in Los Angeles, proposed to re-use the London Bridge stone in facing a new bridge within a new town development (all by private enterprise) situated alongside the Colorado River at a place called Lake Havasu City, an attractive area of Arizona being recovered from the desert to be used to house 100,000 people in a new self-supporting city. The bridge will span from the mainland to a small island in Lake Havasu (the Indian name for Blue Water – and well named), this island to be itself created by severing the neck of a peninsula, after the bridge has been rebuilt – a unique concept within a bold project, the satisfying creation of a living city from desert land."

A LONDON BRIDGE
MISCELLANY

THE GREATEST JOUST IN HISTORY

Various historical novelists of the Sir Walter Scott *genre* have given us graphic accounts of joustings which were not infrequent in earlier days. There was, however, nothing fictional about the famous London Bridge joust; it was a very real thing, well documented in factual terms at the time. Its story presents an epitome of chivalry, patriotism and valour, and it was born of an argument in Scotland between the Earl Crawford of that country and the Lord Wells of England, the latter being Richard II's ambassador to Scotland. The best account we can find is from the pen of the Scottish historian Hector Boethius (not to be confused with the Roman philosopher and statesman Boethius – or Boetius – although he wrote it in Latin). Here is the account:

"During the general peace between the Scots and the English, many of the English, who were of knightly rank, and who excelled in military arts and prowess, frequented Scotland, and there also came many Scots into England; producing, on both parts, many honourable tournaments, to which mutual challenges were published. Of these feats, the most worthy of memory was accounted that victory on London Bridge, by David Lindsay, Earl of Crawford. An Englishman, the Lord Wells, was then the ambassador of King Richard in Scotland and was attending at a solemn banquet, where many persons, both Scots and English, were discoursing on courage and arms.

" 'Away with this strife of words,' said the Englishman: 'whoever would experience the valour of the English, let his name be declared, and also a time and place be appointed, wherever ye list, for a single passage of arms, and I am ready. I call on thee,' said he to Sir David [earl of Crawford], 'who has spent many words against me, and thou shall have to joust with me rather than all the rest.' 'Yea, truly,' said David, 'and I will do it blythely, if thou canst bring the King to consent to it.' The King agreeing to it, the Englishman made choice of the place, and, because it should be in another country, he selected *London Bridge*; David named the time, the holy St George's Day, because he was the chief patron of soldiers. Thereupon the Lord Wells returned to London, and David provided himself with arms, as well he might. As the day was approaching he made a journey with thirty-two persons [actually twenty-nine] in his train, immediately to London, coming to King Richard, who received them with great honour."

It would be interesting to learn where Earl David and his retinue were housed pending the day of conflict, but one assumes they dwelt in some selected premises under the patronage of the king. Certainly the king took a keen personal interest in the trial of arms, and was actually on London Bridge to witness the occasion. For a description of the actual encounter we will turn again to the Scottish historian Boethius:

"When the day of battle was come, both parties being armed, were most honourably conducted to the Bridge, which was filled in all parts with noble spectators, with whom Richard was seated in an eminent place; though a great concourse of the common people also was collected, excited by the novelty of the event, and the fame of the champions. The signal being given, tearing their barbed horses with their spurs, they rushed hastily together with a mighty force, and with square-ground spears, to the conflict. Neither party was moved by the vehement impulse and breaking of spears; so that the common people affected to cry out that David was bound to the saddle of his horse, contrary to the law of arms, because he sat unmoved, amidst the splintering of the lances on his helmet and visage. When Earl David heard this, he presently leaped off his charger, and then as quickly vaulted back without any assistance; and, taking a second hasty course, the spears were a second time shivered by the shock, through their burning desire to conquer. And now a third time were these valorous enemies stretched out and running together; but then the English knight was cast down breathless to the earth, with great sounds of mourning from his countrymen that he was killed. Earl David, when victory appeared, hastened to leap suddenly to the ground; for he had fought without anger, and but for glory, that he might show himself to be the strongest of the champions, and casting himself upon Lord Wells, tenderly embraced him until he revived, and the surgeon came to attend him. Nor, after this, did he omit one day to visit him in the gentlest manner during his sickness, even like the most courteous companion. He remained in England three months by the King's desire, and there was not one person of nobility who was not well affected towards him."

Earl Crawford and his train stayed in London for some three months after the encounter, and one account says that he and Wells became firm friends, greatly to the king's approval. Indeed, such was the chivalry of those days, that the king went to unusual lengths to make the Scottish nobleman feel assured of his welcome. He granted him and his retinue a permit of safe conduct when the time for his return arrived – signed, sealed and delivered to the various sheriffs, mayors, bailiffs and the like who might be involved. Moreover, he put at the disposal of Crawford a ship for the conveyance of his party's armour to Scotland. The ship was the *Sainte Marie*, "whereof William Snelle is Master, with twelve Mariners . . . the said Master and Mariners not carrying with them any property or goods . . . excepting only one complete Armour of War for the body of David Lyndesey of Scotland, Knight. Witness the King at Westminster, the 25th day of May. By Letter of the Privy Seal."

THE WATER-WORKS OF LONDON BRIDGE

It would have been surprising had the citizens of London not made use of the powerful ebb-and-flow currents which surged through the arches of their bridge; yet it was some centuries before this power was seriously utilised. The first water-works were somewhat primitive and used to drive corn mills, mainly to provide meal for the poor. Then in 1582 there appeared upon the scene a Dutchman named Peter Morris (otherwise Morice or Moris), a "naturalised" Englishman if we read aright the description of him as "a free denizen" of London. Morris was the inventor of an "engine" powered by the torrent through the first arch at the City end of the bridge. To prove his point he cast a spurt of water over the steeple of St Magnus' church nearby.

According to Timbs, "Morice used water-wheels turned by the flood-and-ebb current of the Thames through the purposely contracted arches, and working pumps for the supply of water to the metropolis; this being the earliest example of public water service by pumps and mechanical powers which enabled water to be distributed by pipes to dwelling-houses. Previously water had been supplied only to public cisterns from whence it had been conveyed at great expense and inconvenience in buckets and carts."

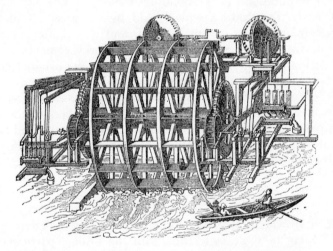

Fig. 8. Peter Morris's water-works at London Bridge.

A grant was given to Morris to extend his invention to other arches – eventually five – and he secured a lease of five hundred years which descended to his family, who drew a good income from it for a century or more. Later they sold both lease and machinery to one, Soames, who secured a new lease and formed a company to "run" the water-works. It was extremely profitable, for every house and public building had to *buy* their water supply. The capital of the new company was in the region of £150,000, in the form of three hundred shares of five hundred pounds apiece. The company supplied thousands of houses and public buildings with water. A water tower had been built on the spot, so that gravity played its part in distributing water by the revolutionary method of pipes. Some of these pipes – those that led over the bridge to Southwark – were of iron, and frequently leaked, thus damaging the stone-work and crowns of the arches. Water-works were eventually instituted over two arches at the Southwark end of the bridge, these being supplemented by a steam engine. Southwark was therefore soon enjoying an uninterrupted supply of water. As to the water-works at the north end of the bridge, these were capable of pumping more than 2,000 gallons per minute, and forcing it up to the second floors of the buildings served.

Clearly, the "subscriptions" paid by the receivers of this service came to an enormous total, and it is significant that when, two centuries later, the water-works came into the possession of "The New River Company", the original company received the then vast amount of £10,000 for the un-expired part of the lease, i.e. some 250 years. Added to this were a number of annuities granted to members of the old company, as well as certain pensions to servants who had been employed by it. With the coming of the new London Bridge, of course, all traces of the water-works in due time disappeared.

"SHOOTING THE BRIDGE"

The narrowness of many of the arches never failed to give excitement to those concerned with the bridge, particularly, perhaps, the folk who had to go under them in boats. With the exception of the central span, which was used for shipping, the arches were so narrow that the water passing through them took the form of rapids, varying according to the tides. So dangerous was "shooting the bridge", as it was called, that it was the custom of many "passengers" in wherries and the like to alight from their boat at one side of the bridge, then walk along the short stretch of Thames Street and rejoin their craft on the other side. It was well said at the time that London

Bridge was for wise men to go over, and fools to go under (plate 9).

The appropriation of several arches to the purposes of the water-works meant that the flood of water through the rest of the arches was fiercer than ever. Another cause of constriction was the constant fortifying, and consequent broadening, of the sterlings – the massive, boat-shaped supports of the piers which held up the bridge.

Curiously, the torrents under the arches were a constant attraction to suicides, and one account states that the dwellers on the bridge were frequently alarmed by the cries of those who plunged into the currents to end their unhappy lives. A notable case of this was that of the son of Sir William Temple, the famous diplomatist and essayist in the time of William III. The son, John, was of great brilliance and achieved the position of secretary of state for war. Owing to the actions of a trusted colleague, however, John Temple felt that he had done some disservice to the king. He filled his pockets with stones and leapt from a boat which he had hired to row him through one of the arches, whereupon, to the amazement of his boatman, he leapt into the rushing torrent, to be seen no more. On the seat of the boat he left a brief letter which has often been quoted. It ran: "My folly in undertaking what I could not perform, whereby some misfortunes have befallen the King's service, is the cause of my putting myself to this sudden end; I wish him success in all his undertakings, and a better servant." The lure of the London Bridge torrents had clearly taken hold of a muddled mind. In the next fifty years there were several other suicides of this pattern – stones and all – but we will not dwell upon them.

THE DOMINANT STERLINGS

The sterlings literally dominated old London Bridge from its inception to its end. They were, as I have mentioned, the massive boat-shaped supports of the piers of the bridge (plates 3, 4 and 9). They also acted as "cut-waters" which protected the piers from the force of the river and diverted it through the arches. They were in constant need of inspection and repair, particularly after a sustained frost when the river flung great

blocks of ice at them during a prolonged thaw. Wherever I have
mentioned these awkward supports I have used the word
"sterling" though there is the alternative spelling of "starling".
Indeed the origin of the word itself is controversial, and the
Chronicles of London Bridge give several interesting possibilities;
among them is the theory that the word is of Danish and perhaps also of German origin. Thus the Danish word *Staer* and
the German *Starr* and *Starck* are linked up with *Stahr* which has
been defined as "a spur to the pillar of a stone bridge, dividing
the water". There was also the suggestion that the word
signified "a defence to bridges"; this appears in an edition of
Dr Johnson's *Dictionary*, though the editor of that edition frankly
admits that "he knows not the etymology", so we will leave the
matter there. As we have shown elsewhere, however, these con-
trivances were an ever present danger to river traffic. Bargemen
were continually complaining that when the tidal water rose
over the sterlings none could tell how deep the water was above
the masonry, so that barges would find themselves "grounded"
thereon and had to await the next tide to be refloated.

"LONDON BRIDGE IS BROKEN DOWN"

... or "falling down" if the reader's recollection of the old rhyme
favours that version. It is, of course, a children's jingle – one of
those repetitive nonsense rhymes which were popular among
youngsters in less sophisticated days than ours. It is certainly
an ancient song, for it is even said that it was alluded to by old
John Stow whose industrious life came to an end as long ago as
1605. It has also been suggested that it dates back to 1282 when
several arches of London Bridge were "broken down" by blocks
of ice during the great frost of that year. The most authoritative
reference seems to have been in an old volume, published in
1810, called *Gammer Gurton's Garland – a choice collection of pretty
Songs and Verses, for the amusement of all little good children who can
neither read nor run.*

No doubt the song was augmented through the years, for it
attained considerable length. The line, "Dance o'er my Lady
Lee" may well have had a link with the River Lee, the ten-
miles-long tributary which flows through Kent to join the
Thames a few miles down river from London Bridge. The

ubiquity of this old song is amazing. Even today the mention of London Bridge in almost any area of England will evoke a cheerful quotation of its first line – "London Bridge is broken (falling) down". It might be well to let the reader be more acquainted with this literally immortal rhyme, so here is one version of it:

London Bridge is broken down,
    Dance o'er my Lady Lee;
London Bridge is broken down,
    With a fair lady.

How shall we build it up again,
    Dance o'er my Lady Lee;
How shall we build it up again,
    With a gay lady.

Silver and gold will be stolen away,
    Dance o'er my Lady Lee;
Silver and gold will be stolen away
    With a gay lady.

Build it up with iron and steel;
    Dance o'er my Lady Lee;
Build it up with iron and steel,
    With a gay lady.

Iron and steel will bend and bow,
    Dance o'er my Lady Lee;
Iron and steel will bend and bow,
    With a gay lady.

Build it up with wood and clay,
    Dance o'er my Lady Lee;
Build it up with wood and clay,
    With a gay lady.

Wood and clay will wash away,
    Dance o'er my Lady Lee;
Wood and clay will wash away,
    With a gay lady.

Then we must set a man to watch,
    Dance o'er my Lady Lee;
Then we must set a man to watch,
    With a gay lady.

Suppose the man should fall asleep?
  Dance o'er my Lady Lee;
Then we must put a pipe in his mouth,
  With a gay lady.

Suppose the pipe should fall and break?
  Dance o'er my Lady Lee;
Suppose the pipe should fall and break?
  With a gay lady.

Then we must set a dog to watch,
  Dance o'er my Lady Lee;
Then we must set a dog to watch,
  With a gay lady.

Suppose the dog should run away?
  Dance o'er my Lady Lee;
Suppose the dog should run away?
  With a gay lady.

Then we must chain him to a post,
  Dance o'er my Lady Lee;
Then we must chain him to a post,
  With a gay lady.

Then build it up with stone so strong;
  Dance o'er my Lady Lee;
Huzza! 'Twill last for ages long,
  With a gay lady.

A little wearisome, we must admit, but nevertheless amusing. One matter eludes us, and that is how the song, in whole or part, with the same tune, and so essentially London, should have become popular throughout the whole of England.

OLD JOHN STOW: THE LOVABLE HISTORIAN

The reader will have noticed in the foregoing pages various references to the works of John Stow – as will the readers of many other books on old London, to the writers of which Stow has been a veritable *vade mecum* since he laid aside his last quill pen in the reign of James I. His main work was his endearing and enduring *Survey of London*. When we consider John Stow, incomparable depicter of his London, we come to a man who wrote as often about what he saw and knew as about what he read. How well he put it in his dedication of one of his histories: "What London hath been of ancient time men may see here, as what is now every man doth behold." His writing is as much enlivened by *is* as retrospected by *was*.

Stow wrote mainly from observation and immediate research. He began life as a tailor and ended it as a recipient of alms, having put aside his original calling for the study of his beloved City of London. He lived humbly and died poor. One can imagine him returning from an exploration, scraping the city mud off his shoes, settling down in his humble home in Aldgate (or, later, by Leadenhall), taking up his quill pen and, by candlelight, scratching down words destined to beguile you and me four hundred years later.

And here it should be mentioned that all his explorations were made on foot, for he was too poor to afford a horse. Speaking of his Survey he said, "It cost me many a weary mile of travel, many a hard-earned penny, and many a cold winter's night of study." He also mentioned elsewhere: "This day I have walked across London and back to verify a fact which, if I put it into my work rightly, would be passed over, but which, put in wrongly, would cause a great stir against me."

The fact that Stow was a "recipient of alms" long ago gave rise to the story that he was forced to beg for his bread. What really happened was that James I, by Letters Patent, authorised him to receive money from those whose admiration of him prompted them to give it. Here are the terms of the Letters Patent:

"Whereas our loving subject John Stow (a very aged and worthy member of our City of London) this five and forty years hath to his great charge, and with neglect of his ordinary means of maintenance (for the generall good, as well as of posteritie as of the present age) and published diverse books and chronicles . . . and therefore we, in recompense of these his painful labours, we have been pleased to graunt our Letters Patent, authorising him, the said John Stow, and his deputies, to collect among our loving subjects, their voluntary contributions and kinde gratuities. . . . We have therefore thought it expedient in this unusuall manner, to recommend his cause to you, having already, *in our own person*, and of our own special grace, begun the largesse for the example of others. Given at our palace of Westminster."

Stow was buried in the church of St Andrew-under-Shaft where Leadenhall Street and St Mary Axe are joined, where there is a monument to Stow in which he is seen writing with his quill pen. Each year, on his anniversary, admirers and civic dignitaries attend a service in the church where a "Stow" sermon is preached, and a new quill pen placed in the cold hand of his mellowed monument. The fact that this charming monument was erected by his widow surely confutes the oft-repeated story that he was eventually forced to "beg for his bread".

Historians who have quoted the works of Stow have frequently referred to him as "dear old Stow". Perhaps the reason for this may be found in the words of Edward Howes, his literary executor:

"He was tall of stature, leane of body and face, his eyes small and crystalline, of a pleasant and cheerful countenance. Though the world smiled not on John Stow, though his toil and study brought him no higher reward than the esteem of good men, and the approval of his own conscience, Providence, in its mercy, had gifted him with a humble, lowly, and religious spirit. He knew full well that 'gain' was not 'godliness', but that 'godliness with content is great riches'; and that knowledge deprived his poverty of its sting, and old age of its fretfulness, and enabled him to live not merely a cheerful but a 'merry old man'."

FISHMONGERS' HALL

This imposing building is the headquarters of the Fishmongers' Company, one of the foremost of the City livery companies (plate 24). It has two claims to inclusion in this book; firstly that it is a neighbour, being almost on London Bridge itself, and secondly that there reposes in it the actual dagger with which Lord Mayor Sir William Walworth stabbed the rebel Wat Tyler, as we can read in our chapter "Rebels at the Gate". In the hall may also be seen a fine statue of Sir William, dagger

in hand, carved in elm in the sixteenth century (plate 27).
Likewise in the hall is a large, impressive arm-chair made from
one of the original piles of old London Bridge (plate 26). Its
motif is various aspects of the bridge.

The present magnificent hall was built in 1831, though it was
preceded by two earlier halls, one of them being burnt down
in 1666 and rebuilt in 1671. The nominal function of the livery
company named above is to examine all the fish brought into
Billingsgate market nearby.

ST MAGNUS THE MARTYR

This is the historic church which stands to the left of the
northern approach to London Bridge and almost adjacent to it.
A church has stood on this site for at least a thousand years;
that is to say that several churches have preceded the present
one, the chief of which was that destroyed by the Great Fire in
1666. Our St Magnus of today, like St Paul's itself and many
other City churches, is an outstanding example of the genius of
Sir Christopher Wren. There is a very small churchyard
attached to it which was once part of the roadway to the old
bridge of Peter de Colechurch.

The tower, supposedly one of Wren's three best, is notable
for its projecting clock, about which an amusing story is told.
It was given in 1709 by one Charles Duncombe who, when an
apprentice, was once thrashed for arriving late for work. The
fact that there was no clock to keep him up to time availed him
nothing, so he made a vow that if ever he became lord mayor of
London he would erect a clock on the church to preserve later
apprentices from meeting the same fate. And, sure enough, he
did become lord mayor and duly erected the clock which we
see today.

The interior of the church, as might be expected of a Wren
edifice, is of extreme beauty. Of special note are the sanctuary
rails which were cast in Sussex, no doubt at the Lamberhurst
foundries which made the imposing tall railings round St
Paul's. These railings (sometimes wrongly maligned) represented almost the last output of the old Sussex foundries, so, as
Wren built both churches, our attribution to Lamberhurst of
the St Magnus sanctuary railings is probably not far wrong.

The connection between St Magnus' church and London Bridge was sustained over many centuries; indeed we mention in Chapter 3 of this book that one of the houses on old London Bridge was the domicile of certain clergy of this church.

There is some uncertainty as to which St Magnus is the patron saint, for there are said to be as many as twenty saints of that name. Many have had a guess at it. It seems likely, however, that he was St Magnus the Viking who was martyred in the twelfth century and buried in the Orkneys. He is described as being loved for his piety and love of peace. A life-size statue of him in the church, however, shows him holding a fearsome-looking battle-axe, shining and keen-edged; he is also equipped with the horns, characteristic of the Vikings. In all it is a noble statue.

A COLOURFUL BRIDGE TAX

In 1249 the custody of the bridge, up to that time in the hands of the City, was transferred to the Exchequer. A score of years later Henry III presented it to his wife, the unpopular Eleanor of Provence – unpopular mainly for the number of foreign favourites she brought into this country, and for her parsimony. This was the Eleanor mentioned earlier who was pelted with stones and mud from the bridge when she set off by water from the Tower to Windsor.

Eleanor had allowed London Bridge to lapse into a sorry state, and in 1281 Edward I ordered a country-wide levy to provide money for the general restoration of the bridge. But sufficient money was not forthcoming, so Edward issued a charter to London Bridge in the form of a Patent of Pontage, or Bridge Tax, thus: "The King to his beloved Mayor and Sheriffs, and to his other Citizens of London – Greeting. Know ye, that in aid of restoring and sustaining of the Bridge of London, we grant that from this day and until the complete end of the three years next following, the underwritten customs shall, for that purpose, be taken of saleable goods over the Bridge aforesaid and of those which pass under the Bridge, that is to say . . . [here I give a few extracts from the extremely long list of items]:

"Of every hundred-[weight] of almonds and rice for sale,

one penny. Of every hundred of pepper and ginger, cinnamon, frankinsense, quicksilver, vermilion, two pence. For every *timbria* [a Norman law phrase for a quantity of skins] of wolves' skins for sale one halfpenny. For every hundred of fir boards, coming from parts beyond the seas for sale, two pence. Of every ship-load of sea-coal for sale, six pence. For every horse for sale, of the price of forty shillings or more, one penny. For every thousand salted herrings for sale, one farthing. For every hundred pieces of sturgeon for sale, two pennies . . . etc."

The reader hardly needs reminding of the differing money values, then and now!

BIBLIOGRAPHY

Survey of London, John Stow (1598).
Chronicles of London Bridge, "An Antiquary" (1839).
Knight's *London* (1851).
Curiosities of London, John Timbs (1885).
Harben's *Dictionary of London*.
A Journal of the Plague Year, Daniel Defoe.
A Chronicle of London 1399–1547, Edward Hall (1548).

St Bride's Library, Fleet Street.

INDEX

ACKNOWLEDGEMENTS

For permission to use the illustrations in this book the author and publishers are indebted to: *Sport and General*, pls 25, 30; *Woodyer Photography*, pls 26, 27; *Mansell Collection*, pls 1, 4, 7, 8, 11, 19, 20 and figs 3 & 4; *The Times*, pls 15, 24, 31, 32, 33; *The Daily Telegraph*, pls 34, 37, 38; *Mary Evans Picture Library*, pls 10, 17, 16, 22 and fig 8; *Barnaby's Picture Library*, pl 12; *The George Inn, Southwark*, pl 28.